*An Introduction to
the Study of Behaviour*

An Introduction to the Study of Behaviour

DAVID McFARLAND
Fellow of Balliol College, Oxford

JILL McFARLAND
Institute of Experimental Psychology, Oxford

BASIL BLACKWELL · OXFORD

631 12050 5 paper
631 12040 8 boards

Printed in Great Britain by Alden & Mowbray Ltd
at the Alden Press, Oxford
and bound at the Kemp Hall Bindery

Contents

To our Parents

Preface

The study of behaviour is a pursuit which is open to any person able to observe animals or fellow humans. In addition to being an exercise in observation and experiment, it is a discipline which demands an objectivity of thought that contradicts man's natural prejudices.

This book is an introduction to the types of thinking and the methods of investigation required by the objective study of behaviour. No prior knowledge of science is necessary, as the book is not intended to be a science text, but rather an introduction to the biological and philosophical issues raised by the study of behaviour.

It is hoped that this book will be used as a meeting point for arts and science sixth-formers and will serve as a general introduction to the human sciences.

The authors wish to express their appreciation to all who have taken an interest in the preparation of this book; and especially to Clifford Henty and Peter Wright for their comments on parts of the text, and to Michael Argyle, Hilary Callan and William McGrew for providing useful material.

We are grateful to the following for permission to use copyright material from the sources shown:

Time-Life International for Figures 1 and 4, from *Animal Behaviour*.

Scientific American Inc., for Figure 10, from *Scientific American*, May 1967.

Part I—Animal Behaviour

1 Why Study Animal Behaviour?

It is not surprising that humans, as members of a social species, should be interested in the behaviour of their fellows. But why should man be interested in the behaviour of other species? In certain circumstances, it is obviously useful for him to learn about the behaviour of animals. Hunters, fishermen and farmers, for example, benefit greatly from understanding the habits of the animals from which they gain their livelihood. Urban man, on the other hand, has no necessity for such contact, and yet continues to express interest and pleasure in the company of animals of many kinds. The fact that so many people keep pets, visit zoos, and indulge in similar purely recreational activities, suggests that interest in animals is deeply embedded in man's nature.

Animals living in close association with man often behave as if men were members of their own species. Heini Hediger of Zürich Zoo has observed that male kangaroos often behave as if the upright posture of the keeper were a challenge to fight. The kangaroo's aggressiveness can be appeased if the keeper adopts the bowed posture characteristic of peaceful kangaroos. Similarly, many people treat animals as if they were human beings. The poodle with its human name, nail varnish, and hair style, is an obvious example. Human visitors to zoos constantly remark on the human-like behaviour of the animals they see there. This tendency to attribute human characteristics to animals is called anthropomorphism (Greek—*anthropos*, man; *morphe*, form). It probably results from an instinctive recognition of morphological and behavioural patterns which provide a foundation for human social behaviour. For example scientists have shown that infant head shape is an important factor in invoking parental responses in human adults. Niko Tinbergen has pointed out that such responses can also be aroused by similar characteristics in young animals, shown in Figure 1, and by Walt Disney cartoons, where such features are exaggerated.

Although man is quick to recognise animal behaviour as human-like, he is reluctant to admit that his own behaviour is animal-like. Man's deep-rooted tendency to see himself at the centre of the

11

FIGURE 1. Common characteristics of juveniles illustrated here include short faces, high foreheads and rounded head shape.

Universe makes it difficult for him to realise his insignificant place in nature. The unpalatable scientific revolutions have generally been those which appeared to challenge man's self-esteem. In 1543 Copernicus started a train of scientific thought in which the Earth was no longer the centre of the Universe, but merely one of many planets moving around the Sun; and Darwin's theory of Evolution by Natural Selection, published in 1859, crystallised scientific thought into a pattern in which man is seen as an integral part of the animal kingdom. Both these developments aroused widespread opposition amongst contemporary educated people. Even today, many people are reluctant to recognise their psychological affinity with animals.

The scientist studying animal behaviour must always keep in mind the fact that he is an animal himself. His motivation and rationale for studying behaviour and his interpretation of observations will all be influenced by anthropomorphism. Asked why he studies animal behaviour the scientist may give an answer similar to that given by George Mallory, when asked why he wished to climb Mount Everest: 'Because it is there.' This rather unsatisfactory answer can be taken as a reference to man's insatiable curiosity about nature, but is probably given by a mountaineer because he does not know the answer to the question. The student of behaviour, however, is used to asking 'why' questions about animal behaviour and may therefore be in a better position to ask them of himself. In attempting to answer 'why' questions about behaviour it is important to recognise that a number of answers may be required to cover all facets of a question.

Consider the question 'Why study animal behaviour?'. We might first explain why we study animal *behaviour* as opposed to animal physiology or animal genetics. The answer here is that zoologists have long studied animal morphology, evolution, physiology, etc., and have recently realised that animal behaviour is not a special 'psyche' subject, but can be studied scientifically as an integral part of zoology. Species differ in their behaviour as in their morphology and geographical distribution. A central problem in evolution is the formation of new species, and it has recently been shown that behavioural differences between sub-species are very important in their further differentiation into separate species. Next we may explain why we study *animal*, as opposed to human, behaviour. This question can be answered from two points of view by distinguishing between the motivation and rationale for studying animal behaviour.

Psychology is not sufficiently advanced to explain adequately what motivates man to scientific study in general. Innate curiosity, a subconscious love of power and a desire to bring order into apparently disparate phenomena have all been suggested. Some scientists will say that they study animal behaviour simply because they love animals, while others like to use animals in the laboratory but would never keep them as pets. Anthropomorphism plays a large part in sentimental attitudes towards animals, and such attitudes can easily result in misinterpretation of animal behaviour. In 1961 the Americans launched a chimpanzee, called Ham, on a suborbital trip into space. When the space capsule was opened on its return to earth Ham was photographed grinning widely and the Press concluded that he had enjoyed his trip. However, Gilbert Manley, who studies the facial expressions of chimpanzees in different situations, has pointed out that chimpanzees grin when frightened and Ham had probably found the experience most unpleasant. When the scientist sees an animal behave in a human-like way, he must guard against immediately attributing human motivation or emotion to the animal. This task is perhaps more difficult for the animal-lover, reluctant to think of his animals as little machines. But there is another side to the coin. The scientist who is really in sympathy with his animals can arrive intuitively at an hypothesis which the analytical mind may never reach. Scientists living in close association with animals, or keeping them as pets, often use their own emotions as a guide to the animal's motivational state. This approach can have value in pointing to initial hypotheses, but these must be followed up by a large amount of experimental and analytical work. Thus we can see that scientists of differing personality are likely to approach a problem in different ways. This generalisation probably applies to all types of scientist, but is particularly pertinent to the student of behaviour because the nature of his experimental material can easily arouse emotions which drive him to one extreme or the other. The history of experimental psychology abounds with examples of failure to maintain a balance between the over-mechanistic and the sentimental or introspective approach. A good student of behaviour will try to understand his own motivation for doing his work, even if he cannot, as yet, obtain much scientific guidance for this complex subject.

We must now distinguish between the motivation and the rationale

for studying animal behaviour and a simple example will perhaps
help to make the distinction clear. A mother pushing a pram is often
seen smiling, making faces and talking baby-talk to the occupant.
Asked why she does this, the mother might answer, 'Because I love
him', 'Because he looks so pretty', or 'Because he is smiling at me'.
Such answers indicate that the baby is an effective stimulus for
releasing the mother's parental motivation. But what is the use of
such behaviour? The mother probably would not know how to
answer this question. It is unlikely that she would reply 'I do it
because I think it is the best way to teach him the English language',
although an educated woman might attempt a *post hoc* rationalisation
of this type. The behavioural scientist, on the other hand, does ask
this type of question and distinguishes between the *use of* and the
motivation of behaviour. It is known that infants deprived of maternal
care often have psychological disturbances in later life, which suggests that the mother instinctively provides an ingredient necessary
for normal psychological development. Thus we can say that the
mother's behaviour is 'useful' to the species, and that this is a 'reason'
for her doing it, even though she may not be aware of it. In this way
a distinction is made between the *cause* of the behaviour, i.e. the
mother's motivational state and the baby's smile, and the use or
function of the behaviour, i.e. the maintenance of a normal and
necessary parent–child relationship. This distinction will be elabor-
ated in the next chapter.

Returning to the original question, 'Why study animal behaviour?',
it is evident that, in functional terms, this is the same as asking in
what ways the study of animal behaviour benefits man. This does not
necessarily mean that the behavioural scientist works with any such
end in view, any more than the mother talks to her baby in order to
facilitate its psychological development.

Although animal behaviour may be studied with no practical
application in view, and knowledge for its own sake is the rationale
applied by some scientists, such knowledge is often found to have
practical value in retrospect. In a sense, therefore, purely academic
study can be identified with long-term practical aims. But not all
animal behaviour studies are embarked upon in this way. For
example, as a preliminary to establishing the Serengeti National
Park in West Africa, scientists made detailed studies of the migratory
behaviour of zebra, wildebeeste and other indigenous species, so
that the boundaries of the park could be arranged to contain and so

protect the herds throughout the year. Man himself can benefit from the study of animal behaviour through its application in the fields of agriculture and medicine. For example, Margaret Vince recently discovered that when young quail are near to hatching they make 'clicking' noises in the egg which speed up the development of neighbouring, more recently layed eggs, so that the clutch tends to hatch simultaneously. Artificial 'clicking' also accelerated hatching, a technique that might be of considerable use to poultry farmers. Experiments with cats have shown that, although they will not normally drink alcohol, they can become addicted to it if subjected to distressing situations. Similarly, a monkey, which received mild electric shocks for making wrong decisions about a simple task, developed gastric ulcers, whilst its partner which received the same shocks, but did not have to make decisions, remained healthy. These examples point to basic causes for these well-known conditions in man and such animal experiments provide a method of investigation that is not open to clinical practice.

Animal behaviour can be directly relevant to the study of human behaviour and many scientists who are primarily interested in humans spend most of their time experimenting on animals. This is because experimentation on humans is often very difficult and sometimes impossible, but many such experiments can be made on animals. In experimental studies of learning, for instance, reward or punishment is usually essential. Animals are often deprived of food for a day or more prior to the experiment and a food reward is given for a correct answer to the problem and perhaps a mild electric shock for an incorrect answer. Such deprivations or punishments would be unacceptable in human experimental work. Similarly, the effects of the administration of drugs, or of alterations to the nervous system, can be studied in animal experiments with much less foreknowledge of the consequences than are acceptable for human studies. Genetical studies are much more feasible with animals than humans: the relatively short life-cycles allow many generations to be studied, individuals can be selected for breeding at the will of the experimenter, and the conditions under which the animals are reared can be carefully controlled. Control of environmental variables is of paramount importance for many experiments and will be explained in detail in Chapters 3 and 5.

This use of animals by scientists who are primarily interested in human behaviour does, however, raise new problems. To what extent is it possible to extrapolate from knowledge of animal behaviour to hypotheses about human behaviour, and in what ways can such hypotheses be tested? These problems will be discussed in Chapter 6, but at this stage it is useful to examine the relationship between man and animal.

In the Western world the Bible was the main authority for the ancestry of mankind until the close of the eighteenth century. But by the end of the nineteenth century most educated people believed that humans had evolved from some non-human ancestor. This revolution in thought was initiated by the work of biologists such as Jean Baptiste Lamarck, Charles Darwin, Alfred Russell Wallace and Thomas Huxley. Darwin's *Origin of Species* (1859) involved man only by implication, but in *The Descent of Man* (1871) Darwin explicitly argued that man and apes have descended from a common ancestor. The popular, but mistaken, version of this view, that man has descended directly from present-day apes, was probably responsible for much of the opposition which Darwin's theories aroused. Feelings at the time are reflected in the exclamation of an English lady: 'Descended from the apes! My dear, we hope it is not true. But if it is, let us pray that it may not become generally known.'

In 1856 relics of primitive types of men were discovered at Neanderthal, in Germany. Since that time, the discovery of many hundreds of fossils has given anthropologists a fair idea of the evolution of men and apes from an early primate stock, although the picture is continually changing as more discoveries are made. Figure 2 gives a rough picture of the evolutionary history of the primates. Similarly, zoologists have been able to trace phylogenetic relationships throughout the animal kingdom (Figure 3). These figures illustrate the distinction between modern representatives of a group and the ancestral form which is no longer living. Modern man cannot have descended from modern apes, because the apes themselves have been evolving during the many millions of years of man's evolution. Recent fossil evidence suggests that the common ancestor of men and apes lived on the ground and walked on two legs. The apes then became specialised for living in trees, while men specialised in other directions.

In attempting to assess the extent to which behavioural studies of animals are relevant to human behaviour, it is important to take into account the phylogenetic relationship between man and the animal concerned, and also the extent to which the behaviour in question is

B

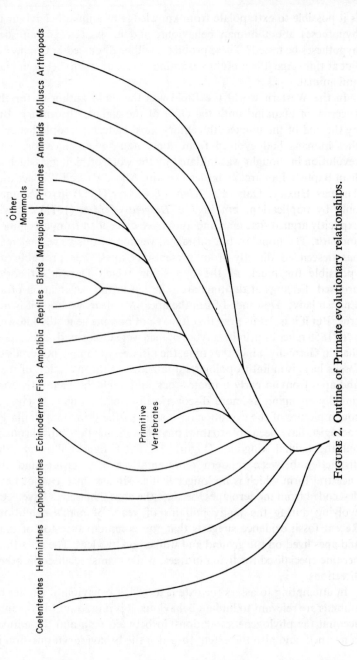

FIGURE 2. Outline of Primate evolutionary relationships.

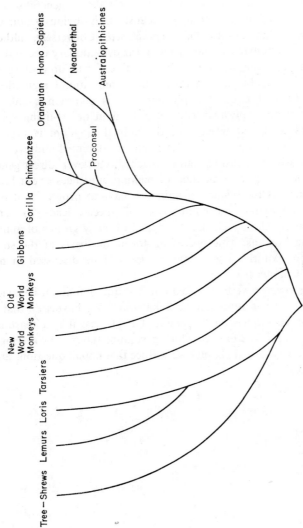

FIGURE 3. Outline of evolutionary relationships within the Animal Kingdom.

specialised. For instance, the close relationship between chimpanzees and humans would suggest that they have many behavioural traits in common. It would, however, be a mistake to generalise about arboreal behaviour, for example, because this is obviously a direction in which chimpanzees have specialised. Conversely, although pigeons and humans are far apart on the evolutionary tree and their common reptilian ancestor has been extinct for millions of years, it may be reasonable to generalise about behavioural regulation of water intake, because the phenomenon is common to all land vertebrates and only markedly specialised in desert-living species. Clearly intimate knowledge of the animal kingdom is necessary before generalisations of this type can be attempted and even then only tentative conclusions can be reached. However, direct generalisation is not the only method of making inferences about human behaviour. As the science of animal behaviour progresses it is becoming apparent that comparison of species leads to certain behavioural rules which can be applied to many groups of animals, including humans. This procedure forms the basis of the subject called Comparative Psychology, which will be discussed in more detail in Chapter 6.

In this chapter we have asked our first question about behaviour; 'Why do humans study animal behaviour?' We have seen that this is not an easy question to answer, but at least it is a reasonable question to ask and one for which general methods of answering are available. In the next chapter we will see that not all questions are so accessible.

2 Asking Questions about Behaviour

This chapter is concerned with those aspects of behaviour which are open to scientific inquiry. First it is useful to distinguish between the metaphysical and the scientific approach to the study of behaviour. The metaphysical approach consists in building theories based on assumptions which may be unverifiable. For example, Sigmund Freud (1856–1939) postulated that the total human personality consists of three major systems—the id, the ego and the superego. The integrity of Freudian theory depends on the assumption that these three propositions are true, even though they are not empirically verifiable. The scientific approach is often said to require no metaphysical propositions. This is not strictly true, because in believing that an experiment repeated under identical physical conditions will always yield the same results, the scientist is assuming that the Laws of Causality (that every event has a cause) will always hold. But as David Hume (1711–76) pointed out, the proposition that the Laws of Causality will operate in the future is unverifiable. Thus the scientist must make an act of faith about causality, and his approach is *sensu stricto* metaphysical. Nevertheless, a distinction can be made between the scientific approach, in which every assumption, except that of causality, is open to empirical verification, and the metaphysical approach, which may involve many unverifiable assumptions.

Insistence on empirical verification excludes from scientific inquiry certain types of question about behaviour. For instance, suppose we wish to know whether animals can experience pain. We can present a stimulus which would be painful to a human and observe the animal's response. We might find that the animal withdraws from the stimulus and avoids the stimulus situation in the future. However, as we cannot ask the animal about its feelings, we have no means of knowing whether it consciously experienced pain. Such withdrawal and avoidance behaviour could be shown by a man-made robot. Can we be sure that animals are not like such machines?

Because of the anatomical and physiological similarity between humans and some animals, it might be argued that we have no right to assume that animals cannot feel pain. However, this is a moral rather than a scientific issue, because we have no empirical means of verifying the theory that animals do have conscious experience similar to ours. As scientists, therefore, we are not able to ask whether animals consciously experience pain, love, hate, etc. In fact, we have no means of determining whether humans have similar conscious experiences to one another. For example, how can I know that, when I see a red pillar box, I have the same subjective experience of redness as you do when you see the same red pillar box? The fact that we both describe the colour in the same way shows only that we have both learned to associate certain personal experiences with the word 'red'. We are not able to verify empirically the theory that subjective experiences are the same for any two people. The fact that humans communicate with one another by means of language is of little help in answering questions about subjective experience or consciousness, because we are not justified in asserting that language is essentially more reliable than any other overt behaviour in conveying such information.

For a long time verbal reports of subjective experience were used indiscriminately as scientific material. However, this 'introspective' method of investigation proved so unreliable that many psychologists rejected the method and purported to rely solely on observation of overt behaviour. This approach has proved very fruitful, although it is doubtful, for the reasons outlined in Chapter 1, whether scientists rely absolutely on objective criteria in forming theories about behaviour. This does not mean that scientists never use verbal reporting as experimental data. After all, speech is a form of overt behaviour, open to the same methods of investigation as non-verbal behaviour. Thus, when a human subject in a colour-vision experiment reports that two colours appear to him to be matched, he provides evidence about the colour-vision process, the reliability of which can be assessed by comparison with the reports of other subjects. A theory formulated from these reports will not involve consciousness, but merely state that a number of human subjects behaved as if the colours were matched.

As important as the way in which the scientist obtains his evidence is the use he makes of that evidence in forming hypotheses. Thus the scientist takes the view that all overt behaviour can be used as evidence, but that the use made of verbal behaviour should not be different in principle from that made of other types of overt behaviour. Having restricted the scope in this way, it may be argued that many of the more interesting questions, such as those about states of consciousness, are not open to scientific investigation, and that such an attitude takes the *psyche* out of psychology. A distinction should then be made between the study of behaviour as a science and the study of psychology as a branch of philosophy. Although this book is concerned with the former, deterministic approach to the subject, it may be interesting to ask what can be said about consciousness from such a viewpoint.

A good test of the deterministic attitude is to ask the following question. Suppose it were possible to construct an exact physical analogy of oneself, either from the same biological hardware, or perhaps from electronic material, so long as every physical state in the human had an exact counterpart in the model. The question is, would the model have the same conscious state as the human? The true determinist would have to say that it would. However, it would not be possible to determine whether the conscious state was the same or not, just as it is not possible with a fellow human. So the determinist can only make an act of faith that the model would be the same as the human in every respect.

Because the deterministic attitude to behaviour is objective, it excludes questions about subjective perceptual or emotional experiences. Nevertheless, much the same ground is covered by the two approaches. Thus, if we ask why a man is shouting, or a dog barking, it is not useful for the scientist to answer 'Because he, or it, is angry', except where the word 'anger' is used as a shorthand for a set of observable phenomena. The scientist claims that in describing the set of circumstances which causes a man to shout or a dog to bark, he is providing a complete explanation for the behaviour, even though it may not be an explanation that the layman could reconcile with his everyday subjective experience. The type of scientific explanation given for such behaviour patterns would depend very much on the way in which the scientist looked at the question. This point is well illustrated by the following example:

a. Why do birds sit on *eggs*?
b. Why do birds *sit* on eggs?
c. Why do *birds* sit on eggs?
d. *Why* do birds sit on eggs?

Clearly, by emphasising different parts of the question, different types of answer would be appropriate. Thus, in type *a* the implied question is, 'Why do birds sit on *eggs*, rather than on stones or flowers?' To answer this aspect of the question it would be necessary to show what stimulus characteristics of the egg, such as its shape, colour, and markings, were important in eliciting the sitting response. In other words, what characteristics of the egg are important for the bird to recognise it as an object-to-be-sat-on. Investigations of this type sometimes give surprising results. Thus, Niko Tinbergen showed that a brooding Herring Gull, given a choice between two artificial eggs, one of normal size and one much larger, prefers the larger egg (see Figure 4, opposite). The reasons for this are not yet fully understood.

In type *b* the emphasis is transferred to the observation that birds sit on, rather than stand on or eat their eggs. Here the answer must be given in terms of the animal's motivation. Thus birds sit on eggs when they are broody but may eat them when hungry. The scientist must define what he means by broody and what by hungry, and this task will usually involve knowledge of the physiology of the animal. Brooding birds are characterised by an increased amount of the hormone prolactin in the blood. Prolactin is released from the pituitary gland after participation in nest-building and courtship. The presence of the hormone is a necessary but not a sufficient condition for a bird to respond to an egg in the appropriate way, because, as we have seen, it is also necessary for the egg to provide the correct stimulus characteristics. Thus question *b* can be seen to be causally complementary to question *a*.

Question *c* implies causality of a different order. Why do *birds*, rather than cats or pigs, sit on eggs? The answer is that birds have an hereditary predisposition to produce eggs and to develop the machinery for responding to them appropriately. The genetic factors involved can be regarded as long-term causal factors necessary for the appearance of the behaviour. The manner in which such traits are handed from one generation to the next provides the material for the important science of behaviour genetics. Although much of an animal's behavioural repertoire is determined by heredity, a large amount is acquired during the animal's lifetime. The process of acquiring such behaviour patterns through experience, called learning, is as important as heredity in answering questions of type *c*. Suppose the question had been, 'Why do humans (rather than other animals) write on walls?' The type *c* answer would be in terms of

FIGURE 4. The large egg is preferred to the egg of normal size.

learning rather than heredity, because a human is not born with the ability to write, but acquires it during its lifetime. However, the distinction between learned and innate is not a rigid one. For example humans inherit the ability to learn to write, and no other animal, however intelligent, has this ability. Moreover, many behaviour patterns, such as bird song, develop as a result of complex interaction between the genetic and learning processes. Thus the answer to the type c question should not be seen in black and white, learned or innate, but as an answer to the question: How was the behaviour pattern established in the animal's repertoire?

In answering the type d question, we might say that birds sit on eggs in order to hatch them. This statement need not imply that the birds anticipate the consequences of their behaviour, but merely that the behaviour is necessary for the production of the next generation, and only birds that are 'programmed' to behave in this way leave offspring. This type of argument, first put forward by Charles Darwin in his *Origin of Species*, states that the survival value of any inherited trait is determined by Natural Selection. That is, the extent to which a trait is passed from one generation to the next, in a wild population, is determined by the breeding success of the parent generation and the value of the trait in enabling the animals to survive natural hazards, such as food shortage, predators and sexual rivals. Such environmental pressures can be looked upon as selecting those traits which fit the animal to the environment. This is what Darwin meant by 'survival of the fittest'. Behavioural traits are just as important as morphological and physiological ones in determining the survival of the species. Thus each behaviour pattern has a function related to the survival of the species, and it is often important for scientists to know what that function is.

The functional significance of birds sitting on eggs is directly related to the survival of the species, because eggs must be incubated if the young are to hatch, but the function of many behaviour patterns is not so obvious. For example, Black-headed Gulls remove the broken egg shells from the area of the nest when the young have hatched. What is the function of such behaviour? It is evident that there must be a strong survival value, because in leaving the young to carry away the shell, the parent is exposing them to predation. By careful experiments, scientists have shown that an important function of egg shell removal is that it helps to maintain the camouflage of the nest. In these experiments, sixty Black-headed Gull eggs were placed, singly and widely scattered, in close vegetation near to the gullery. Each egg was partially camouflaged with a few straws of Marram grass and half the eggs were marked by a broken egg shell placed near by. Observations showed that predatory Carrion Crows and Herring Gulls found the marked eggs much more easily than the eggs which had no broken shells near by. This work shows that ideas about the survival value of behaviour need not be purely conjectural, but can often be investigated experimentally.

We have seen that, in answering questions about behaviour, the scientist can take several points of view. In general, psychologists are more interested in the mechanisms that control behaviour, *a* and *b*, and zoologists in how the mechanisms came to be as they are, *c* and *d*. However, a complete answer to a 'why' question should cover all aspects of the problem and the different approaches are often of mutual benefit. For example, Karl von Frisch questioned the validity of experiments which purported to show that bees were colour-blind, on the grounds that such a conclusion implied that the bright colours of flowers pollinated by bees had no functional significance. Based on this question, Von Frisch carried out a series of experiments which demonstrated conclusively that when looking for food bees do discriminate colours. Indeed, some flowers, that appear unpatterned to humans, have a pattern of ultra-violet radiation that can be detected by bees. Thus by asking different types of question scientists assist the work of one another.

3 A Typical Problem

To demonstrate some of the methods used in the study of behaviour we will now discuss a typical problem: How can we determine what an animal sees?

Everyone is familiar with the verb 'to see' but its everyday usage is too imprecise for thorough behavioural investigation. The examples below will illustrate this. Suppose two children each have an orange in the left hand and are throwing a ball between them and catching it with the right hand. Either player can throw his orange and the object of the game is to catch the ball but not the orange. If the ball is thrown rapidly backwards and forwards a large number of times, then one player suddenly throws his orange, the other will often catch it automatically. We may say that the child must have seen the orange in order to catch it, yet in the sense that he did not distinguish it from the ball we might say that he did not really see it, otherwise he would not have caught it. As another example, a stream of cars along a motorway may appear to one person as a long line of cars of different colours, sizes and shapes, but to another will be Fords, Triumphs, Vauxhalls, etc. The cars seen are the same, but the impressions they make on the two observers are quite different.

It is helpful to consider an animal as living in three concentric worlds. The outermost is the physical world which includes all that is possible for an animal to detect. Inside this is the world which the animal is capable of perceiving and this world is different for different species. For example, humans have a rather limited visual range within the total spectrum of radiation, and their range is slightly different from that of bees which are able to detect ultra-violet radiation, but are more limited at the red end of the spectrum than is man. In other sensory modalities there are also large differences. Thus birds have a relatively poor sense of smell and mammals an acute one. For any one species the world of capability can move about within the physical world through evolutionary change. For instance, certain nocturnal moths, which are preyed upon by bats, have developed the ability to hear the very high frequency pulses emitted by flying bats. This extension of their auditory capability enables the moths to take avoiding action when they hear an approaching bat. Man has extended his visual world by providing himself with artificial extensions to his sense organs, such as telescopes and X-ray detectors.

Inside the world of capability is another which consists of information which is responded to, or stored for future reference. Here we are distinguishing between what an animal can see and what it does see in any particular circumstance. Experiments have shown that animals often fail to respond to visual stimuli which their sense organs are perfectly capable of detecting. For example, David Lack observed that male Robins often attack other red-breasted Robins which trespass on their territory. They will also attack a stuffed Robin placed in the territory, but only if it has a red breast. It appears that the red breast is a powerful stimulus for labelling another Robin as an intruder. Indeed, Lack showed that a territory owner would vigorously attack a bunch of red feathers, just as if they were an intruding Robin. No one doubts that a Robin is capable of distinguishing between a bird and a bunch of feathers, but in the territorial defence situation Robins appear blind to all attributes except the red breast.

The factors which determine what an animal sees within its world of capability are complex and involve many aspects of its psychological make-up. Scientists have shown that many animals have an innate predisposition to respond to certain aspects of a stimulus whilst ignoring others. For example, the newly hatched chicks of many seagulls peck at the red spot at the tip of the parent's bill and so stimulate the adult to regurgitate food. Experiments have shown that red spots are more effective than spots of other colours and that other aspects of the parent's head and bill are relatively unimportant. In the laboratory animals have been trained to respond to stimuli other than those they naturally respond to, showing that they are capable of seeing such stimuli. In nature, too, learning by everyday experience is an important means by which animals come to recognise stimuli. For example, Konrad Lorenz showed that many young animals learn to recognise their parents during their first few weeks of life. An animal's motivation or mood is also important in determining what aspects of a stimulus it responds to. Thus, bees, given a choice of coloured lights, fly towards the brightest when frightened but when hungry they choose the colour which they have learned to associate with food.

To summarise, we can say that what an animal sees in any situation depends on its visual capabilities, inborn tendencies, past experiences and present mood. All these factors must be considered by scientists investigating what animals see.

There are four main methods used in the study of animal vision. These are: (1) anatomical investigation, (2) physiological analysis, (3) interference with the animal's natural environment and (4) training animals to discriminate between visual stimuli.

Anatomical investigation is an appropriate starting-point, because a good idea of the visual capabilities of an animal can often be obtained by studying the anatomy of its light-detecting organs. In some animals these are so rudimentary that they are only capable of distinguishing between different intensities of light. Earthworms, for example, have many simple photoreceptors scattered over the body surface. These can detect changes in light intensity and, as their nocturnal habit suggests, earthworms avoid high illumination. Some animals which have taken to living underground, or in caves, have eyes which have degenerated from a more highly evolved state. Moles, for example, have retained enough of an eye to tell light from dark, but cannot distinguish patterns. For pattern vision it is necessary to have either a lens, as in most vertebrates, or a compound eye made up of many little eyelets, as in insects and crustacea.

Eye size and shape also give information about an animal's visual capabilities. Eyes with a large pupil and lens are advantageous for nocturnal animals so that they can pick up as much light as possible. Such eyes are found in the Opossum, House Mouse and Lynx (Figure 5). In other nocturnal animals, such as owls and bush babies, the limitation on lateral expansion by the skull has led to tubular extension towards the back of the head. These animals have very restricted eye movement and have to turn the head instead. Many owls, for example, can turn their heads through 270 degrees. Fish which live in the deep sea, where there is very little light, often have eyes similar to those of nocturnal animals (Figure 5). Studies show that nocturnal and dim-light vision are characterised by high sensitivity, but low ability to discriminate detail and the facility for colour vision is often lacking. Not only do the size and the shape of an animal's eyes give us some indication of its visual abilities, but so also does their position in the head. Predatory animals often have the eyes facing forwards, giving binocular vision, which improves depth and distance judgment. Animals which are preyed upon, such as

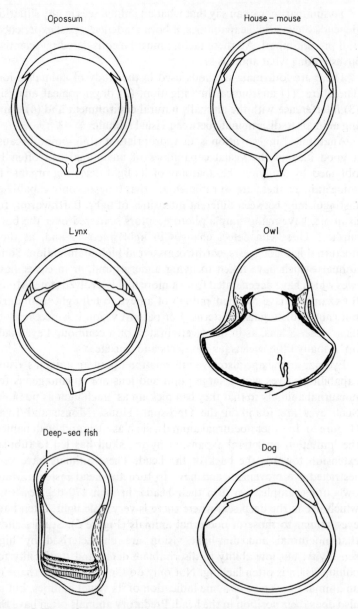

FIGURE 5. Eyes of nocturnal animals compared with those a of dog, which has both day and night vision.

rabbits, have laterally placed eyes, which give a wider visual field and thus a better chance of spotting an approaching enemy.

The eyes of diurnal animals generally have low light sensitivity, but are capable of high visual resolution in good light. Resolution of detail is increased by a specially sensitive area of the retina called the *fovea centralis*, which is present in many highly visual fish, reptiles, birds and primates. The fact that primates are the only mammals to have such foveae suggests that detailed vision is rather poor in other mammals. Animals that are active both by day and night have a mechanism for regulating the amount of light reaching the visual cells. This is done either by changing the size of the pupil, through which light enters the eye, or by movement of the pigment in the retina.

The above examples illustrate that examination of the gross structure of the eye can be a guide to an animal's visual capabilities. The detailed anatomy of the eye can also give many clues about animal vision. Examination of the retina has revealed two types of photosensitive cells, which are termed rods and cones. Cones are known to be essential for colour vision and good visual resolution, and studies have shown that they are numerous in the eyes of diurnal animals. Rods are more sensitive than cones and it has been found that the eyes of nocturnal animals often contain only rods.

It should now be clear that the value of anatomical investigations is that they contribute towards our knowledge of the physical capabilities of an animal's visual apparatus. The second method of investigation, physiological studies of the eye and brain, provides similar information. Physiologists can record electrical changes in the optic nerve, through which messages are transmitted from the eye to the brain and some recordings have been made from the brain itself. By such methods scientists are able to determine what colours and shapes the eye can respond to and they may one day be able to build up a complete picture of what an animal is capable of seeing. However, the techniques involved are extremely difficult and progress is slow. So far behavioural methods give a more reliable picture of an animal's visual capabilities.

Selective interference with the animal's environment has proved a productive way of making a preliminary study of animal vision. The aim of the experiments is to change aspects of the environment in such a way that any change in the observed behaviour can be attributed to the environmental change. For example, experiments with the carnivorous water beetle *Dytiscus marginalis*, which has well-developed eyes and good visual capabilities, have shown that vision is not used for catching prey. Tadpoles placed in a test-tube were ignored by the beetle, whereas those in a muslin bag were immediately attacked. It is known that *Dytiscus* has well-developed chemoreceptors and the experimental results suggest that the beetle uses chemical stimuli to detect prey underwater, although it is known to respond to visual stimuli in other situations. Preliminary investigations are often possible in the field, but it is usually necessary to bring the animal into the laboratory to study its visual processes in detail, so that adequate controls can be introduced into the experiment.

A controlled experiment is based on the rationale that all variables should be kept constant or their effects known, except those that the experimenter is deliberately manipulating and recording. The necessity for controls is well illustrated by the example of 'Clever Hans', the horse that amazed the German public at the beginning of this century by his ability to answer questions on mathematics, spelling and other aspects of the school curriculum. Hans answered questions by tapping his right forefoot to indicate numbered letters or words on a blackboard, or as a direct answer to mathematical questions. He could handle most schoolboy arithmetic which did not involve prolonged and tiring tapping. Although some people suspected trickery, Hans's owner, Herr von Osten, was quite sincere and Hans had a high success rate when questioned in the owner's absence. In scientific circles Hans's achievements caused quite a stir and Oskar Pfungst and other psychologists from the University of Berlin undertook to investigate the matter. They found that Hans could answer questions put to him in French, but had difficulty in answering questions to which the answer was one and always failed when the questioner did not know the answer himself. Thus, if one man whispered a number and another questioner, not knowing the first number, whispered another number to be added to the first, then Hans could not give the correct answer. Hans also failed in the growing dusk and when wearing blinkers. As a result of his investigations Pfungst concluded that Hans watched his questioner very carefully and stopped tapping when the human gave some involuntary signal, such as a small muscle twitch or a change of breathing. Even questioners who knew which cues the horse used often had difficulty in suppressing them. This example shows how careful one has to be in experimenting on animal behaviour. In laboratory experiments it is now standard practice to take precautions against tricks of the type used by Clever Hans and these precautions are called controls. The following example will illustrate the method.

Suppose we wish to determine whether rats can distinguish between red and green hues. A suitable procedure would be to arrange for the rat to choose between two coloured lights. The apparatus could consist of a Y-shaped box with the entrance at the base of the Y and a coloured light at the end of each arm of the fork. But before lights are introduced into the box it is necessary to allow the rats to accustom to the apparatus and experimental procedure. The usual training is to deprive the rats of food or water in their home cages and to reward them appropriately for each choice in the experimental box. The coloured lights are then introduced and the choice of only one of the colours will be followed by a reward.

Before starting the experiment we must ensure that any other aspects of the rat's environment, which might be used as a cue to reward, are controlled. The experimenter must make sure that he cannot be seen by the animal or heard placing the reward on the correct side. The reward itself must not be visible or provide olfactory cues. If the choice is to be between two hues, care must be taken to ensure that the animal is not able to respond on the basis of brightness or saturation differences between the lights used. This cannot be done by making the brightness and saturation physically the same for the two stimuli, because a colour-blind animal's brightness sensitivity is not the same over the whole spectral range. For this reason the brightness and saturation of the stimuli have to be varied so that no one property except hue can be associated with reward. The two stimuli must not always be at the end of the same arms, otherwise the rat could simply learn to go to the right or to the left every time. Changes in position, brightness, etc., should be made in a random order to prevent the animals responding to a pattern of changes. Rats can learn, for example, to run to the right on alternate trials.

Having eliminated all other cues, we are now in a position to test whether rats can distinguish between red and green hues. If the choice of red is followed by reward and, after a number of trials, the rats consistently run towards the red light, we can conclude that they are capable of the discrimination. Should the rat not learn, however, the experimenter would not know whether the rat could not discriminate the stimuli, or was simply not intelligent enough to learn this type of

C

task. In practice this difficulty is often avoided by choosing a task appropriate to the animal's known learning capabilities. For example, it is almost impossible to train frogs to choose between coloured lights to obtain a food reward. But these animals will demonstrate certain colour preferences in an escape situation, and this method has been successfully used in the study of frog colour vision.

In this chapter we have seen that a typical problem of animal behaviour can be tackled by several different methods. Behaviour students need to be aware of the contribution that can be made by anatomists and physiologists, but in the study of behaviour, the ultimate tests must be in terms of behaviour and the two main approaches to this problem will be discussed in more detail in the next two chapters.

4 Studying Animals in their Natural Environment

The value of studying animals in their natural environment was appreciated relatively late in the history of animal psychology. Although naturalists and a few scientists, such as Henri Fabre (1823–1915), studied animals in the field, most studies during the first third of this century were conducted in the laboratory. The pioneering work of Konrad Lorenz and Niko Tinbergen in the 1930s attracted the attention of many scientists and led to the development of the ethological approach to behaviour. The ethologist's attitude to behaviour studies differed markedly from that of most contemporary animal psychologists. While the former emphasised the species-specific aspects of behaviour, the latter attempted to discover general principles of behaviour by studying a single species, usually the laboratory rat. During the last twenty years there has been a considerable *rapprochement* between the two schools of thought, so that it may soon be possible to talk about a unified science of behaviour. However, it will be useful to discuss the main interests of the ethologists, before going on, in the next chapter, to the study of animal behaviour in the laboratory.

The main arguments embodied in the ethological approach to behaviour may be summarised as follows:

1. Much animal behaviour is species specific and highly integrated with the animal's normal environmental circumstances.

2. It is therefore appropriate to study animals in their natural environment as we cannot expect to observe an animal's full range of behaviour in the laboratory.

3. Although it is possible to employ a rigorous scientific method in the experimental study of behaviour in the field, this should be preceded by a thorough descriptive analysis of the behaviour of the species concerned.

4. Investigation of the functional relationship between an animal and its environment is important for a proper understanding of the behaviour observed.

5. Because behaviour has evolved, studies of behavioural similarities and differences between animals can help in their classification and facilitate an understanding of behaviour mechanisms.

This chapter will be concerned with the further elaboration of these five points.

In Chapter 2 we learned that much of an animal's behaviour repertoire is determined by heredity. At the gross level this observation is an obvious one. Thus birds can fly and pigs cannot. However, scientists have shown that many fine details of behaviour are also influenced by the animal's genetic make-up. There is evidence that small differences in courtship behaviour are of prime importance in preventing interbreeding between closely related animal populations. As interbreeding is the main criterion by which species are distinguished it follows that such behavioural differences must be species specific. Failure to interbreed, however, halts the interchange of genetic material between the two populations, so that their genetic character begins to diverge and their genetically influenced behaviour becomes more and more dissimilar. In addition to genetic mechanisms, group-specific behaviour can be maintained by cultural mechanisms, by which information is passed from one generation to the next through learning. Cultural mechanisms operate most commonly in humans, but also exist in other animals. The opening of milk bottles by tits is a learned ability which is maintained in this way. Experimental work has shown that the development of the normal song of passerines such as the Chaffinch, Blackbird and Meadowlark, is dependent on imitation. When these birds are reared in isolation they develop only a very simple type of song.

As much behaviour is species specific, extreme care must be taken in drawing conclusions about the behaviour of one species from observation of another species, although, as explained in Chapter 1, we can expect behavioural similarities between closely related species. The way in which the behaviour of closely related species diverges depends on the differences between their environments. The process of Natural Selection, outlined in Chapter 2, ensures that an animal's behaviour is closely fitted to its environment. Only when we study an animal in this environment can we hope to observe the full range of its species-specific behaviour. Descriptive analyses of behaviour observed in the field provide information about the stimuli that an animal responds to and are a valuable preliminary to experimental work in the field and to more detailed studies in the laboratory. Some behaviour patterns observed in the laboratory would be difficult to understand if they had not also been observed in their natural context. For example, ducks and gulls in captivity sometimes show foot trampling on a damp cage floor. This apparently incongruous activity has been observed in the wild by Niko Tinbergen to be part of the normal feeding behaviour, serving to stir up food in shallow water. Sometimes behaviour patterns which would normally occur in nature are completely absent in the laboratory. For instance, many pigeons and doves breed perfectly well in the laboratory without displaying the complicated aerial flights which are part of their breeding behaviour in their natural environment. Laboratory conditions may produce abnormal behaviour, that is, behaviour rarely or never observed in the field. For instance, birds kept in too small a cage, or fish in too small a tank, are often much more aggressive towards each other than under natural conditions. This is particularly true of animals, such as doves, which have no special mechanism of appeasement by which an inferior individual can prevent attack from a social superior. Konrad Lorenz has described how a dove attacked and killed its cage-mate which under normal circumstances could have escaped. It has also been found that animals bred in the laboratory for many generations may develop a behaviour repertoire which is quite different from that of their wild relatives. For example, Anthony Barnett has noted that the exploratory behaviour of laboratory rats is quite different from that of their wild relations. While the former show little hesitation in investigating unfamiliar objects, the latter are extremely cautious and generally avoid regions of their territory which are suddenly changed. Such observations justify the ethologist's claim that field studies contribute valuable information towards an understanding of animal behaviour.

When we study animals in the field it is important to ensure that our presence does not disturb them. For this reason the field worker often constructs a small viewing tent, known as a hide. The hide may be camouflaged with pieces of vegetation and has one or more slits through which the animals are observed. Most animals accustom to the presence of such a structure and after a while continue with their normal behaviour. At the field station at Ravenglass on the Cumberland coast, hides are set up in the Black-headed Gull colony in the dunes and it is usual for the observer to be accompanied to the hide by another person who then departs. As long as the gulls see someone both arriving at and leaving the hide, they quickly settle down after the initial disturbance. Modern ciné cameras and tape recorders are an invaluable aid to field workers. On film there is a complete and permanent record of the behaviour which was observed. Slowing down the film allows analysis of the components of behaviour patterns which normally occur too quickly for the eye to follow, and may involve social interactions. If you have tried to describe in words the calls of birds, you may well appreciate the value of tape recorders. Again the record is permanent and available for further analysis. Sound spectrographs, which give a precise physical description of a sound, have proved especially useful for comparing the vocalisations of closely related species. In this way it has been possible to distinguish between calls made by the starlings resident in Washington and those in New York. It was also discovered that the birds themselves can tell the difference; Washington starlings were not frightened by the alarm calls of their New York cousins, which were broadcast in an attempt to scare them off the city buildings.

The use of the ciné camera has also opened up a whole new horizon to people in general, through the media of cinema and television. You may be familiar with the wild-life films, which are not only of scientific interest, but also have great popular appeal. The work of Jane van Lawick-Goodall has shown that it is not always necessary to study animals from a hide, even in the forests of Africa. Instead, she went to live amongst the chimpanzees she wished to study and photograph. No doubt tempting morsels were provided to encourage the chimps to overcome their fear and stay in the vicinity, a technique you may have used to bring birds into your garden. On film Jane van Lawick-Goodall has an exciting record of the life of a family of chimpanzees under entirely natural conditions. One aspect difficult to cover when making this film was the social behaviour of the apes moving as a group through the jungle. This brings us to the problem of animal movement. Many animals travel vast distances, and various techniques have been used to discover their routes and destinations. The ringing of birds is a familiar example and a similar technique has been used to plot the movements of fish. Radar is used to follow migrating birds and in Africa the movements of herds of game have been studied from the air. Experiments have shown that birds removed to a strange environment, hundreds of miles from home, can return in a remarkably short time. It is known that they are able to navigate using the sun's position in the sky, but the exact nature of the cues they use is still a mystery.

These techniques facilitate a detailed description of behaviour observed, the first stage of a field study, and from this the scientist may be able to form a preliminary hypothesis. The hypothesis then has to be tested and there are three main ways in which this can be done in the field. These are: (1) by statistical analysis of the observations, (2) by interference with the animal's environment and (3) by the use of models which more or less resemble natural stimuli. Statistical analysis can be used to determine whether different activities tend to occur together, or periodically, and what reliability can be attached to such conclusions. For such analyses to be of value a large number of observations must be available. Thus, after his preliminary observations, the scientist will often go back into the field and make an exhaustive study of those aspects of the behaviour which he thinks important. This can be an extremely tedious business as field observations cannot be speeded up. It may involve hours in a hide waiting for the animal to show the behaviour in question, or, when studying breeding behaviour, for example, it may be necessary to wait for a whole season before further observations can be made.

In Chapter 3 experiments designed to investigate the prey-catching behaviour of the water beetle *Dytiscus marginalis* were described to illustrate the method of selective interference with the environment. This method can also be used in the field. For example, Niko Tinbergen observed that the female Digger Wasp, after hunting afar for food for her larvae, finds her way back to her own burrow in the colony. He carried out a series of experiments to determine which features of the environment the wasp used to locate its burrow. Wasps were trained to return to a burrow around which a circle of pine cones had been arranged. If, during one of the wasp's subsequent trips, the circle of cones was moved about a foot away from the burrow, she returned to and searched within the circle of cones, ignoring her burrow near by. Similar experiments showed that the wasps may learn about other details of the environment, such as small stones or tufts of grass. A wasp given a choice between a circle of stones and a triangle of cones chose the circle of stones, showing that the arrangement of the objects, rather than the objects themselves, may be the feature which the wasp learns about.

An approach which has proved very rewarding for field workers is the use of models, which more or less resemble natural stimuli. Thus an assortment of long thin objects, painted to resemble in varying degrees the bill of an adult, was used to investigate the pecking response of newly hatched gull chicks. Stuffed specimens of owls and foxes have been used to study reactions to predators and stuffed or completely artificial conspecifics to study reaction to territory intruders. The use of models has the advantage that the stimulus can be presented at the will of the experimenter, who can also alter the configuration of stimuli which he presents to the animal. Such techniques have provided information about the environmental stimuli, called sign stimuli, that an animal is responding to at any particular time.

We can now turn to the fourth of the ethological arguments outlined on page 35, that investigation of the functional relationship between the animal and its environment is important for a proper understanding of behaviour. In Chapter 2 we saw that scientists distinguish between the cause and the function of behaviour and that the concept of function is related to the Darwinian argument of Natural Selection and survival of the species. An example of experiments performed to investigate the survival value of a particular behaviour pattern is the investigation of egg shell removal by Black-headed Gulls, described in Chapter 2.

Why, you may ask, is it important to know about the survival value of behaviour? Surely it is enough to know about its present-day causation, without bothering about the reasons for the evolution of the behaviour. Some scientists do indeed hold this view, but others claim that the study of function can aid the understanding of causation. For example, many scientists believe that certain facial expressions used for communication by mammals, including man, have evolved from protective responses. When in a potentially dangerous situation, they protect their delicate sense organs by such movements as lowering the eyebrows, pushing back the ears and raising the hair around the head and neck. Such movements give potential information to other animals, who can interpret them as signs of fear or anger. These primitive facial expressions provide good material for the selection of an efficient communication system. Thus, where it is advantageous for animals to recognise each other's motivational state, Natural Selection will act to make existing facial expressions more effective as a means of communication, so that they come to serve a double function. The expressions can be made more effective in a number of ways. Thus, many birds have specially marked or coloured plumage which serves to emphasise the ritualised (exaggerated) movements used in communication. The absence of hair on the human face is thought to serve a similar function, by emphasising the main features used in communication. Expressions are also made more effective by what Charles Darwin called the Principle of Antithesis. Figure 6 shows that the posture of an angry dog is in many ways the opposite of its posture when friendly. Similarly, human facial expressions indicating pleasure and anger use opposing sets of muscles.

Knowledge of the primitive function of facial expressions can greatly help the understanding of communication in animals and man. The grinning of a frightened chimpanzee (Chapter 1) is an illustration of a typical protective response (preparation to bite) and is probably close to its primitive form, whereas in man, who usually grins and smiles in pleasant situations, the response is highly evolved. The earlier function of the human smile is perhaps illustrated by the ingratiating smile, often given to social superiors, and by the fact that some people grin reflexly when frightened in a social situation.

In Chapter 2 we described how Karl von Frisch's speculation about the function of flower colours led to the discovery of colour vision in bees. Another instance of the fruitfulness of this line of thought followed from von Frisch's curiosity about the function of the dance of foraging bees on returning to the hive. Von Frisch's investigations not only showed that the dance directs other bees to the food source, but also led to the discovery of the ability of bees to detect the plane of polarisation of daylight (the plane in which light waves vibrate).

Let us now consider the fifth aspect of the ethological approach to behaviour. Appreciating that behaviour has evolved, ethologists have obtained a great deal of information from comparative studies of animals. Comparison of the behaviour of different species provides a further method by which hypotheses based on field observations can be substantiated. For example, the hypothesis that egg shell removal in dune-nesting gulls serves a camouflage function is reinforced by the observation that Kittiwakes, which nest on cliff ledges and are therefore less exposed to predation, do not remove the broken egg shells after hatching.

Comparison of species can also give clues about the motivation of a behaviour pattern. For example, most gulls when simultaneously aggressive and frightened adopt a 'threat' posture characterised by

FIGURE 6. Darwin's Principle of Antithesis illustrated by the posture of a dog when friendly (*above*) and angry (*below*).

an upright carriage with the neck held vertical and the bill pointing downwards. The wing carpels, or 'elbows', are held away from the body and the feathers are sleeked as is usual in frightened birds. The exposed carpels could indicate readiness to fly away (fear) or to beat an opponent with the wing (aggression). However, carpel exposure is common in the aggressive postures of other species which use wing-beating during fighting, whereas the Great Skua does not use wing-beating and does not raise the carpels during threat. The evidence obtained by comparison of species, therefore, suggests that raising the carpels during threat has a primarily aggressive motivation.

Behavioural differences between closely related species relate to differences in way of life. For example, Kittiwakes, though phylogenetically close to other gulls, show behavioural peculiarities associated with the cliff-nesting habit. Esther Cullen has suggested that their relative freedom from predation is probably responsible for the following characteristics: The adults are very tame while on the cliff ledges, only giving alarm calls or fleeing when potential predators are very close; they do not attack predators as other gulls do; neither the eggs nor the chicks are camouflaged; the nest, made conspicuous by the adults who defecate just over the rim, becomes even more conspicuous when the young hatch, because the parents do not remove the broken egg shells. Because of the danger of falling off the cliff, Kittiwake chicks, unlike those of dune-nesting gulls, do not run when alarmed. Kittiwake parents, like other gulls, feed their chicks by regurgitating food, but they do not drop the food on to the ground but feed the chicks directly from the mouth, so that fouling of the nest is avoided.

Behavioural similarities between species may be due to close phylogenetic relationship, or to evolutionary convergence due to similar habitat or way of life. Thus, pigeons and Sand-grouse are closely related and have in common a method of drinking by pumping, peculiar to their order. On the other hand, pigeons, in common with other tree-living birds, have a special foot-locking device for gripping perches, while Sand-grouse have the feathered feet characteristic of ordinary grouse, to which they are not closely related. The classification of animals has been principally based on those morphological characteristics which are thought to reflect phylogenetic relationship, but recently it has been realised that innate behaviour patterns can provide a useful way of checking this type of classification. Thus grooming movements and the form of the nest have been used in the classification of some insects and birds, and the form of the web for spiders.

In this chapter we have outlined the ethological approach to animal behaviour and have attempted to show how the study of animals in their natural environment is important for understanding behaviour as a part of the total biology of the animal. This approach brings the study of animal behaviour close to other branches of biology which take an overall view, such as ecology and taxonomy. But the study of behaviour also has an affinity with the more mechanistic biological sciences, such as genetics, physiology and psychology and some of these aspects will be considered in the next chapter.

5 Studying Animals in the Laboratory

Although the study of animals in their natural environment provides important information about the range and variety of animal behaviour, laboratory studies are of prime importance for investigating the mechanisms of behaviour. In Chapter 3 we emphasised the importance of controlled experiments. The variable conditions in the field make this type of experiment extremely difficult, but in the laboratory much of this variability can be excluded.

In bringing animals into the laboratory it is necessary to ensure that they are not disturbed by the alien environment. Some animals, such as fish, can be studied in semi-natural conditions in the laboratory. This is largely a matter of convenience, as it makes selective interference with the environment much easier. However, to conduct a fully controlled experiment, it is usually necessary to study the animal in completely artificial conditions. Although wild animals can be brought into the laboratory and gradually accustomed to the new conditions, a number of advantages are gained from breeding experimental animals in captivity: the animals grow up under similar conditions to those in which they will be studied; the history of each individual is known from birth; an important source of variation can be eliminated by ensuring that all the animals to be used in a particular study are the same age and reared under the same conditions. The number of animals required for a particular experiment is influenced by the variation between individuals. The experimenter must study enough individuals to ensure that his results are statistically reliable and could not have been obtained by chance. Obviously if all individuals were identical it would be necessary to study only a few individuals, as all would produce exactly the same results under the same experimental conditions. This situation is never achieved because there are always genetic differences between individuals, but it can be approximated to by ensuring that the animals have roughly the same experience before starting the experiment.

To illustrate some points of procedure let us return to the experiment on discrimination in rats, described in Chapter 3. We have seen that a rat given a choice of two visual stimuli, only one of which is accompanied by a reward, can learn to choose correctly on almost every trial, provided that it is capable of discriminating the stimuli.

This type of experiment is also widely used to study the learning process, but in these experiments it is necessary to use stimuli that the animal is known to be able to discriminate. A group of animals which had been bred in the laboratory and were known to be experimentally naive would be chosen for the experiment. Suppose that twenty rats was considered a sufficient number to give statistically reliable results. These would be maintained at a constant temperature and artificial day-night cycle. They would be deprived of food (or water) for about twenty-three hours each day, so that they were always hungry (or thirsty) at the start of the daily experimental tests. Initially the rats would be placed in the apparatus each day but not given food there. When they had accustomed to this procedure the learning tests would begin.

Appropriate stimuli for investigating discrimination learning in rats would be a black rectangle versus a white rectangle. It is usual to present these on a grey background and the experiment would incorporate all the normal controls discussed in Chapter 3. Instead of limiting the animal to a single cue, which is essential when investigating sensory capabilities, we could study how the availability of two ways of solving the problem influences the learning process. Thus, the rectangles could be of different sizes or of different orientations. Let us consider the case of brightness and orientation differences, so that if the black rectangle is presented vertically the white one is horizontal. Now we have to decide which stimulus is to be rewarded and which not. Here we run into the problem of confounding the rat's preferences with his learning ability. Thus, it may be that rats find it easier to learn about brightness than about orientation, but that they also prefer black to white. If we reward the black stimulus the rat would already be biased towards the correct choice and would learn the problem more easily than if we rewarded the white stimulus. Thus the rat's initial preferences could easily confound the investigation of his learning abilities. One way of overcoming this difficulty is to divide the twenty rats into two groups of ten, one rewarded for choosing black and the other for white. However, the same problem arises with respect to the orientation cue, so each group should be divided again into halves, one of which is rewarded for choosing the vertical rectangle and the other

STUDYING ANIMALS IN THE LABORATORY

for choosing the horizontal rectangle. Table 1 shows that, with respect to the configuration of the rewarded stimulus, the experiment has a balanced design.

TABLE 1

Group	Number of rats	Orientation of stimulus	Colour of stimulus
1	5	H	B
2	5	V	B
3	5	H	W
4	5	V	W

B = black; W = white; H = horizontal; V = vertical.

To investigate the learning process the rats must be given many trials in the apparatus. Each trial would consist of a choice between the two stimuli, and the experimenter would record whether or not the choice was a correct one. Experience has shown that it takes a naive rat about one hundred trials to learn a problem of this type. Obviously all the trials could not be run on a single day, as the rat would not be hungry after so many rewards and would soon stop running altogether. Ten or twenty trials a day would be a more suitable number and with a group of twenty rats it would be reasonable to run ten trials per day. However, care must be taken to ensure that the rats are run at the same time each day, as it is known that a rat's learning performance is different at different times of day. Performance is generally poor in the afternoon when rats like to sleep. To ensure that each animal is run at approximately the same time each day, and tested both early and late in the daily session, rats one to twenty are run on trial 1 before moving to trial 2. As training continues the rats would gradually improve in performance, as shown in Figure 7. This curve of performance as a function of trials is called a learning curve. The importance of reward in learning is shown by the fact that performance falls off rapidly and eventually ceases, if reward for correct choices is withheld (Figure 7). This decline in performance is termed 'extinction'.

To solve this type of learning problem, rats have to learn which stimulus to approach to obtain reward, and which to avoid. However,

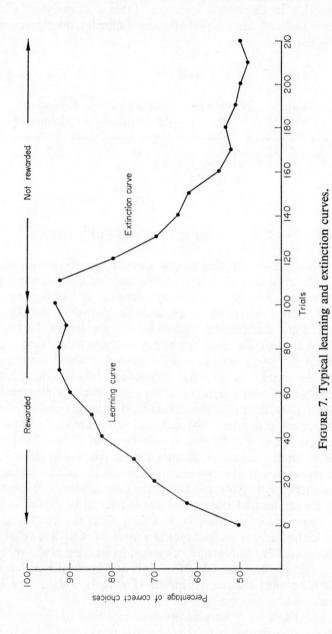

FIGURE 7. Typical learning and extinction curves.

there are many characteristics of the stimuli with which reward could be associated. Thus, the rats could learn to associate reward with the shape, size, position, orientation, colour or brightness of the stimuli. In the present case the rats could never solve the problem on the basis of shape, size, position or colour, because the rewarded and unrewarded stimuli do not differ in these respects, whereas they do differ in brightness and orientation. But how are the rats to discover which stimulus characteristics to associate with reward?

In a brilliant series of experiments Stuart Sutherland and Nicholas Mackintosh have shown that many animals have to learn two things in solving problems of this type: (1) which aspects of the stimuli to attend to, and (2) which of the two manifestations of that aspect is rewarded. For example, a rat which was rewarded on a trial in which it had attended to the brightness of the stimuli would be more likely to attend to brightness in the future; and if the rat happened to choose the black stimulus, it would be more likely to choose black on those future trials during which it attended to brightness. Rats which learned to attend to brightness or orientation, or both, could successfully learn to solve the problem outlined above, whereas rats which attended to other aspects of the stimuli, such as size or position would only be able to obtain 50% reward. Therefore the rats attending to brightness or orientation or both will always be more rewarded.

To determine which aspects of the stimuli the rats have in fact learned to attend to, unrewarded 'transfer tests' can be given. During transfer tests the rats would be presented with the stimuli differing in orientation or brightness, but not both. Thus on half the trials the stimuli would be black or white rectangles differing only in orientation, and on the other half horizontal or vertical rectangles differing only in brightness. Rats which had learned to attend to orientation only would be able to solve the first problem but not the second, while those which had learned to attend to brightness only would be able to solve the second but not the first problem. Rats which had learned to attend to both brightness and orientation would be able to solve both types of transfer test.

Investigation of animal behaviour in the laboratory often involves experiments which are specifically designed to test hypotheses. Typically, the results of preliminary investigations, such as the establishment of a learning curve, lead to the formation of an hypothesis, such as the two-stage learning process outlined above,

D

for which there would generally be a certain amount of supporting evidence available. For instance, the two-stage hypothesis is supported by the results of transfer tests which show that the more rats learn about one aspect of a stimulus, the less they learn about others. The most useful predictions made from an hypothesis are those which are not made by other hypotheses. For example, most learning theories predict that the more animals are trained with stimulus A rewarded and stimulus B unrewarded, the longer it will take them to solve the reverse problem: stimulus A unrewarded and stimulus B rewarded. However, the two-stage hypothesis predicts that prolonged training on the initial problem would make the reversal easier, because the rats would learn more thoroughly which aspect of the stimuli to attend to and this learning would continue to be relevant when the problem was reversed. Nicholas Mackintosh has shown that the predictions of the two-stage hypothesis are correct in this respect and has since gone on to develop the hypothesis into a powerful body of theory, applicable to many different learning situations and to different species.

In the first part of this chapter we have concentrated on a single type of experimental investigation in order to bring out some important principles, such as the use of controls, the design of experiments and the formation and testing of hypotheses. However, there are many other techniques which are used to investigate animal behaviour in the laboratory.

Experiments utilising runways, mazes and discrimination boxes are generally conducted on a trial-by-trial procedure, such as the one described above. Another method is the free-operant procedure, in which the animal is allowed to indulge in some learned behaviour at its own pace. Rats and pigeons have been most frequently chosen for this type of experiment, though many other animals, including humans, have been used. Operant conditioning consists essentially of training a subject to perform a task to obtain a reward. A rat, for example, may be required to press a bar or a pigeon to peck an illuminated disc. The method of training is termed 'shaping'.

Let us consider the training of a pigeon which has to peck an illuminated disc, called the key, to obtain a food reward. After one or two days of food deprivation in the home cage, the pigeon is placed in a small cage equipped with a mechanism for delivering grain, and a key at about head height (Fig 8, opposite). Delivery of food is normally signalled by a small light which illuminates the

FIGURE 8. Pigeon performing in a Skinner box inspects the square illuminated key (*above*), on which a stimulus is projected, pecks it (*above right*), and obtains a food reward delivered into a hopper located below the keys (*right*).

grain. Pigeons soon learn to associate the switching on of the light with the delivery of food and approach the food mechanism whenever the light comes on. The next stage of shaping is to make food delivery contingent upon some aspect of the animal's behaviour. A pecking response is frequently used, but pigeons can also be taught to preen or turn in small circles, for example, by using this method. Pecking is shaped by limiting rewards to movements which become progressively more similar to a peck at the illuminated disc. So when it has learned to approach the key for reward, the pigeon is then rewarded only if it stands upright with its head near the key. At this stage the pigeon usually pecks at the key spontaneously; slow learners can be encouraged to peck by temporarily glueing a grain of wheat to the key. When the pigeon pecks the key it closes a sensitive switch in an electronic circuit which causes food to be delivered automatically. From this point on the pigeon is rewarded only when it pecks the key and the manual control for reward is no longer required. The animal is now ready for use in an experiment. This experimental technique was designed by the American psychologist, B. F. Skinner, and the apparatus is called a Skinner Box.

Many types of experiment utilise this operant conditioning procedure. For example, discrimination learning can be studied by rewarding the animals for responding only when a certain colour or pattern is presented, or by allowing the animal to choose between two keys which are visually differentiated. The technique has proved particularly useful for studying the effect of different types or patterns of reward. Thus, instead of rewarding a pigeon for every peck, it can be rewarded for every nth peck, so that there is a fixed ratio between number of pecks and number of rewards. This procedure is called a fixed-ratio reward schedule. Other common schedules include variable ratio, fixed interval and variable interval. On an interval schedule, reward is given at intervals of time specified by the experimenter. The animal is rewarded for the first response made during a given interval. Different schedules of reward have been found to have different effects on the animal's performance. For example, a variable interval schedule produces a very uniform rate of responding; for this reason it is often used to test the effect of drugs, reward size, etc.

The operant conditioning technique is widely used, not only for purely behavioural tests, but also in physiological investigations. For example, animals with electrodes chronically implanted in the brain have been trained to administer electrical stimuli to the brain by pressing a bar. When the electrode is in certain areas of the brain the animals avoid the bar, while in other areas they press it repeatedly, showing that the electrical stimulus acts as a reward.

Laboratory methods for investigating non-behavioural subjects, such as physiology and genetics are beyond the scope of this book, but it should be realised that much research is conducted in the borderline areas of behaviour-physiology and behaviour-genetics. For example, the mating behaviour of the fruit-fly *Drosophila* has been extensively studied to investigate the way in which genetic make-up affects behaviour. Subtle differences in courtship behaviour have been found to affect breeding rate and choice of mate.

In conclusion we can say that the investigation of animal behaviour in the laboratory is necessary for a science in which hypotheses must be tested experimentally. Although a certain amount of progress can be made in the field, the more sophisticated techniques and the fully controlled conditions which are available in the laboratory are essential for this rapidly developing science.

Part II—Human Behaviour

6 Relationships between Animal and Human Behaviour

The remainder of this book is concerned with the study of human behaviour. But before entering into detailed discussion of this field, it will be helpful to consider some general questions about relationships between animal and human behaviour studies. These can be grouped under three main headings: (1) the interpretation of behavioural observations in the two fields of study; (2) the problem of applying facts and theories about animal behaviour to the study of human behaviour and (3) the applicability, to human studies, of experimental techniques used by students of animal behaviour.

Let us consider questions of interpretation first. In Chapter 1 we saw that observations of animal behaviour can easily be misinterpreted in terms of human experience. Such anthropomorphism has its counterpart in the study of human behaviour. In animal studies there is a danger in attributing human characteristics to animals; in human studies in attributing one's personal feelings to the human subjects being studied. Suppose a human subject is observed giving a door a sharp kick after failing to open it by hand. The observer might assume that the subject was impatient or annoyed, simply because he thinks he would be annoyed in a similar situation. In fact, the subject may have reasoned that a sharp kick would be likely to open the door, without feeling annoyed at all. The scientist must aim at being as objective in interpreting observations of human behaviour as he would when studying animal behaviour. This requirement is often difficult to fulfil, especially when dealing with verbal reports. In Chapter 2 it was argued that there is no scientific basis for regarding verbal reports as a type of evidence different from other types of overt behaviour, and that, as such, they must be treated objectively.

Inquiry into human behaviour should be conducted on the same scientific principles as inquiry into animal behaviour, and therefore, as argued in Chapter 2, the subject matter of consciousness is not part of the subject matter of the science of behaviour. And just as we cannot use the overt behaviour of animals as a guide to their conscious experience, so we should not expect to identify, with reliability, overt behaviour with conscious states in humans.

The foregoing arguments rest on the assumption that man has no special status as an object for scientific investigation. The validity of this assumption may be questioned by theologians and philosophers, but for the scientist the assumption follows logically from his belief in determinism. However, we can legitimately ask whether all the types of answer that can be given to questions about animal behaviour can also be applied to human behaviour. In Chapter 2, the question 'Why do birds sit on eggs?' was used to illustrate explanation in terms of the relevant (i) stimulus, (ii) motivation, (iii) inheritance and (iv) survival value of the behaviour. Do these four types of explanation also apply to human behaviour?

This question is relatively easy to answer for the first three cases. Thus, stimulus recognition, appropriate motivation, and the learned or inherited ability to act accordingly, are just as important in the explanation of human behaviour as they are in animal behaviour. However, it is not clear to what extent questions about survival value are relevant to human behaviour. Although man is a product of the evolutionary process and was at one time subject to the same types of selective pressure as other animals, it has been claimed that man is no longer subject to evolutionary laws. In the long run, man's fate is, of course, tied up with the evolution of the Universe, but at present there is no doubt that man is capable of controlling many of the selective pressures that he would otherwise be subjected to. This fact makes it difficult to recognise the function of many aspects of human behaviour, which now occur in a much changed environment. A second factor which obscures the functional significance of much human behaviour is the immense degree to which the behaviour is determined by learning. It may well be necessary to evaluate the functional significance of human behaviour in terms of cultural rather than biological evolution.

We now come to the problem of the evolutionary relationship between animals and man, particularly as it affects the process of generalisation from animal to human behaviour. In principle this problem is the same as that of generalising from any one group of animals to another. Each animal group shares some of its make-up with other groups, but is also specialised in particular respects. Man can be regarded as an animal specialised for thinking and communication.

In Chapter 1 the evolutionary relationships between various animal groups were outlined, as a basis for generalisation between groups. On the whole, generalisation between phylogenetically closely related groups is most accurate, but the degree of specialisation of the behaviour in question must also be taken into account. Thus, primitive aspects of behaviour are often found to be similar in many groups of animals. For example, most mammals have similar methods of temperature and water intake regulation, which are controlled by a primitive area of the brain common to all. However, the camel, which is specialised for desert living, is able to store heat in the daytime and dissipate it in the cold desert night, and this enables it to economise on cooling by water evaporation during the day to a degree not possible in other species. The widely held belief that camels can store water to a greater extent than other species is fallacious. Thus, it is possible to generalise widely about the regulation of water intake, and it has been found that this type of behaviour is remarkably similar in animals as different as pigeons and rats.

Many species exhibit behavioural specialisations not found in related groups. An example is the ability of bats to detect objects by echolocation. However, similar abilities are sometimes found in relatively unrelated species. For example, echolocation is also well developed in porpoises, in which it has evolved quite independently.

We can expect some primitive and unspecialised types of animal behaviour, such as avoidance reactions and reactions to gravity to be directly relevant to human behaviour. However, such detailed instances are relatively unimportant compared with the general rules that can be formulated from the study of the whole spectrum of animal behaviour. For example, distinctions between learned and innate behaviour, and between external (stimuli) and internal (motivational) causal factors, are of very widespread applicability in the animal kingdom, and can therefore be expected to be applicable to human behaviour. Intensive study of many species has led to the formulation of general rules about the learning process. In Chapter 5 we saw that, as a general rule, discrimination learning in animals can be regarded as a two-stage process in which the animal learns (1) which aspects of the stimuli to attend to, and (2) which of the two manifestations of that aspect is rewarded. Recent experiments on discrimination learning in children between the ages of five and nine have shown that the same process occurs, but learning in older children appears to be more complicated. So rules applicable to animal behaviour may also apply to human behaviour, at least at certain stages of its development.

Konrad Lorenz in his book *On Aggression* speculates about the degree of aggression shown by man, as compared with animals, who do not normally kill other members of their own species. Fighting in social species is prevented by the use of ritualised threat, and Lorenz postulates that this principle also applies to man, but its operation has been disturbed by the development of weapons. This type of interference by cultural factors is a common hazard in applying principles of animal behaviour to humans. However, one important principle, which will be discussed in more detail in the next chapter, is that primitive types of behaviour tend to be superseded, but not abolished, by the development of more advanced and more complex behaviour. Studies of animals and of human infants show that primitive parts of the brain remain in higher animals, but that their action may be interfered with by the parts which developed later in evolution. Thus, the idea that primitive behavioural tendencies are deep rooted in human nature may be true in a very real sense.

Finally, we can ask whether the techniques of conducting behavioural experiments on animals are applicable to human experimental work. The story of Clever Hans illustrates the importance of taking precautions against undesirable alternative ways in which the subject might fulfil the experimental task. Such controls are just as important in studying human behaviour. Many of the particular aspects of controlled experimentation on humans will be discussed in Chapter 8, but some general problems will be mentioned here.

Much of the tedious preliminary training for animal work can be replaced by verbal instructions when humans are the subjects. The experimenter must, however, take care that he does not give his subjects clues about possible results of the experiment, and for this reason its true nature is often disguised. Ideally the subject should not have prior knowledge of the field of investigation. Thus it is not always wise for the scientist to use his colleagues as subjects.

Experimental work with animals has shown that performance is greatly affected by level of motivation, and care is usually taken to ensure that animals are tested at the same motivational level on different occasions. They may, for example, be kept without food for a specified length of time before each experiment. However, with human subjects it is much more difficult to control for motivational level. For example, two schoolboys could be of equivalent intelligence yet score quite differently on an IQ test if one was enthusiastic and the other disinterested.

The design of human experiments can benefit from knowledge of animal experiments. For example, it has been found that animals which have had experimental experience in a similar environment sometimes generalise between the two situations, so that experience of the first experiment can contaminate the results of the second. Regression to behaviour in previous similar situations is particularly common when the subject becomes frustrated by a difficult task. Similar factors could operate in experiments with humans, so that the subject may unconsciously behave in a way relevant to a previous experiment. Such phenomena can also be important in everyday life. There is, for example, evidence that after changing from driving on the left side of the road to driving on the right side, the motorist may regress to previous habits in an emergency.

To summarise we can say that man, as a member of the animal kingdom, is likely to possess many behavioural traits in common with other animals. Nevertheless, great care has to be taken when comparing man's behaviour with that of other species, as he is specialised in certain important respects. Students of human behaviour can certainly benefit from a knowledge of animal behaviour and the experimental designs used in its study. On the other hand, the scientist must remember that he is himself human and therefore liable to the same psychological pitfalls as any other person. These he must guard against; in particular the egocentric assumption that his species is subject to principles of behaviour which are necessarily different from those operating in other species.

7 Studying Humans in their Natural Environment

It is fairly obvious what is meant by the natural environment of animals, but a definition of the natural environment of man is not so easy. For primitive man the environment was comparable to that of animals, but that of modern man might be described as 'artificial' because it is of his own making. But man's environment is just as much a part of nature as is a beaver's lodge or a spider's web, and though it ranges from the Australian desert to the city of New York, such environments are natural for their indigenous populations. This chapter will be concerned with studies of humans in their normal environments, in which the subjects are unaware that their behaviour is being observed; as distinct from investigations, to be described in the next chapter, in which the subject is asked to participate in an experiment. Before considering the behaviour of adults, we will look at the behaviour of children, taking the new-born infant as a starting-point.

The behavioural repertoire of new-born infants is virtually limited to sleeping, feeding and crying. Nevertheless something of great interest has emerged from studies of the new-born; at this stage the human displays certain activities which disappear for ever after a few weeks. For example, new-born, and especially premature, babies show stepping movements which are independent of the body orientation. These movements disappear during the first few months of life, never to reappear in the same form, the stepping movements of normal walking only occurring when the body is in its normal relation to gravity. Similar stepping movements have been observed in animals, such as cats and dogs, in which the higher centres of the brain have been damaged or anaesthetised.

Work on animals suggests a reason for the presence of certain reflexes in infants which disappear after the first few weeks or months of life. The sequence in which different parts of the infant brain start to function is the same as that in which they were formed embryologically. The order of embryological development in turn reflects the evolution of the brain. Thus the 'lower' areas of the brain, corresponding to the brains of primitive animals, develop before the 'higher' areas, which were acquired later in the evolutionary history of man. In the new-born infant the lower areas are functional, but the higher areas begin to function only a few weeks or months after birth. Accordingly certain primitive reflexes, such as the stepping reflex, are present in the new-born and disappear after a few weeks as a result of inhibition by the higher centres.

The grasp reflex is another example of this phenomenon. Touch or pressure on the palm causes flexion of the digits so that the stimulus object is grasped. In a similar reflex, the toes bend around a slender object. The grasp reflex develops before birth and can be elicited during the physician's pre-natal examination. It is so reliable and strong that it is sufficient to support the weight of the whole body for a short time. It disappears six to twelve months after birth but may reappear in brain-damaged adults. The most effective stimulus for eliciting the grasp reflex is a hairy object, which suggests that its phylogenetic significance is to be found in monkeys, which spend their early life clinging to their mother's fur. It has also been suggested that the fact that babies are comforted by rocking movements is associated with the rhythmical movement the infant monkey receives as its mother moves about. Many other infant reflexes, mostly concerned with posture and locomotion, are relics of the behaviour of more primitive animals.

Observations of infant behaviour are carried out systematically both by the pediatrician as part of his routine clinical investigation, and by scientists inquiring into the development of human behaviour. Such investigations have proved to be of great importance in the development of our understanding of child care. It is known, for example, that the smiling response is an important index of the child's emotional well-being, and it has been found that it develops earlier in infants reared at home than in those reared in institutions.

Facial expression in children is much more marked than in adults and illustrates many of the principles of communication outlined in Chapter 4. Darwin's Principle of Antithesis is illustrated by comparing the facial expressions associated with unpleasant stimuli with those observed when the child is attracted to the stimulus. Thus, noxious tastes elicit frowning, eye closing and turning down the corners of the mouth, accompanied by a copious flow of saliva. In addition, head shaking and spitting appear towards the end of the first year. Facial expressions during crying resemble those elicited by a noxious taste; pouting precedes crying and is also shown by infants in expelling milk from the mouth. When looking or listening, on the other hand, young children open both the eyes and the mouth. If a child is asked to open its mouth it also opens its eyes and hands, showing that the different reactions work in unison. It is interesting that blind people similarly open and close their eyes when their other senses are correspondingly stimulated.

The complexity of the behaviour of older children makes systematic descriptive recording difficult. However, Corinne and John Hutt for their studies of child behaviour, devised a special hospital waiting-room and developed a method of study based on those used in field investigations. The children are introduced into the waiting-room which has normal fittings, such as light switches, radiators and a wash basin. On one wall, however, is a one-way mirror, through which the experimenter can watch the children without himself being seen. Each child is left alone for a short time and is free to wander around the room and manipulate objects in the environment. Sometimes toys are introduced so that behaviour in a 'rich' and a 'poor' environment can be compared. A detailed description of the child's behaviour in the waiting-room is made by a trained observer speaking into a tape recorder. Great care is taken to avoid inferential statements. For example, words such as 'anxious', 'happy' and 'angry' are avoided, and replaced by simple statements about the observed behaviour, such as 'stands still, face whitens, lips tremble, fists clenched'. Some psychologists regard such observations as arid, but the Hutts have demonstrated that the method is extremely accurate and reliable. The reliability of the reported observations is periodically checked by comparing the reports from two independent observers and determining the degree to which they are in agreement. At the end of each experimental session a written transcription is made of the tape recording and this is then analysed statistically. The principles behind this method of investigation are therefore similar to those used in animal field studies.

Results from this type of analysis show, for example, that brain-damaged children spend a much shorter period of time at each type of activity than do normal children. The behaviour of brain-damaged children was found to be similar in rich and poor environments, whereas normal children are influenced much more by the change in environment. In a similar type of study, Corinne Hutt and William McGrew found that children showed much more aggressive and defensive behaviour when they were crowded. Such behaviour was frequently associated with possession of toys. In a rectangular playroom possessive behaviour was common under crowded conditions, but territorial behaviour, consisting of attempts to preserve a physical area against intruders, was rare. In a clover-shaped room, however, both possessive and territorial behaviour were common. These findings are remarkably similar to those from studies of animals, which show that increased crowding often results in increased aggression and stress, even if the food supply is plentiful. Overcrowding is rapidly becoming a problem for modern man and the anthropologist, Carleton S. Coon, states that ' . . . the problems of food supply and standing room become insignificant and academic compared with the problem of increased stress and decreasing sanity . . .'. Clearly research into the behavioural effects of high population density is a matter of urgency in view of the present high rate of increase of the human population.

Let us now turn to the study of adult behaviour. Most of the work of a purely observational nature is conducted in indoor environments, such as offices, factories, libraries and waiting-rooms, where the observer can take notes without attracting the attention of the subject. In a library, for example, it is possible to note observations quite openly without arousing suspicion. In factories, offices and waiting-rooms one-way mirrors are frequently employed to enable the observer to operate without being seen by the subject. A technique frequently used is the deliberate interaction of a colleague with the subject. Although this approach is experimental, it is natural as far as the subject is concerned, and thus corresponds to the use of models in animal field work. Providing the subject is unaware that he is participating in an experiment, the study can be regarded as taking place in the natural environment. Social psychologists frequently used to rely on subjective interpretation of the observed behaviour, but recently there has been a trend towards a more objective approach. So having taken precautions against the subject becoming aware that he or she is being studied, the next step is to employ a set of objective and reliable measures of the observed behaviour. For this purpose the behaviour can conveniently be divided into verbal and non-verbal, and we will first consider measures of non-verbal behaviour.

Physical appearance is an important determinant of social behaviour in humans, and is particularly important in the early stages of a social encounter. Certain physical attributes, such as stature, build and pigmentation, are largely genetically determined and the individual can do little to alter them. Other features, such as facial expression, can be partly controlled, while some, such as clothing, are entirely a matter of personal choice. As in other primates, the face is the most important part of the body used in communication, and, apart from speech, the eyes are generally considered to be the most important factor. Eye movement is a measure frequently employed by social psychologists, as it is an aspect of behaviour about which the subject is often unaware. Although eye movements are probably used as a means of communication by many vertebrates, in humans they are especially important and are accentuated by the conspicuous contrast between the white area and the coloured iris. During a conversation between two people eye movements help to synchronise the conversation and can also indicate whether the listener is attending to the speaker. In an analysis of films of two-person interactions, Adam Kendon found that the person speaking looks at the person he is addressing at the end of long utterances, which is the point at which information about the reaction to the verbal message is most needed. The eye movement acts as a signal for the listener to respond. Michael Argyle and his co-workers found that people become disconcerted when the eyes of the person they are talking to are hidden by dark glasses.

Certain aspects of whole-body behaviour, such as posture and proximity, are also important in human social interactions. As in other animals, bodily proximity and contact vary with the degree of familiarity between the individuals and with the stage reached in the social encounter. Greeting ceremonies are used to establish or renew close social interaction, and it is interesting that they are also widespread amongst animals. Under normal conditions the distance between two people is a compromise between the preferences of each. By asking a co-operative subject to remain stationary, Michael Argyle and co-workers were able to study how close other subjects would approach to start a conversation. They found that the subjects tended to stand either two to four feet or nine to twelve feet away from the other person, but rarely four to nine feet. They considered that these results indicate a decision on the part of the subject to enter into an intimate social relationship or to remain at a distance where conversation was only just possible.

Speech is, of course, man's most important means of communication, and both verbal and non-verbal aspects of speech can be measured objectively. The timing of speech has already been mentioned in connection with eye movements. The main measurements employed are the length, the frequency, and the number of utterances and silences. These measures can be manipulated experimentally by an interviewer, who interrupts or remains silent in a standard manner during different phases of the conversation. The subject's reactions to these treatments are recorded by a concealed observer. Studies of the same individual in a series of encounters show that there is considerable consistency in the speed of speech for a given person. This measure is therefore used to indicate what psychologists call 'personality' differences.

The emotional tone of speech can be measured in physical terms, such as changes in loudness and pitch. Correlations between such measures and other aspects of behaviour can be used to indicate the effect of the subject's emotional state on his speech. A typical finding is that speech rate correlates positively with speech errors and that both these correlate with measures of anxiety. It is, of course, extremely important that the investigator should use purely physical measures and avoid subjective assessments in studies of this type.

The verbal aspects of speech have long been studied by linguists, and they, in recent years, have joined psychologists in the development of the important study called psycholinguistics. Grammar, style and choice of words are typical of the subject matter of this science. A mathematical theory of grammar has been developed and this may prove to be important in the handling of language by computers.

The view that verbal behaviour can be studied in the same manner as non-verbal behaviour is reinforced by the fact that the two share many basic behavioural principles. For example, in Chapter 5 we described how pigeon behaviour can be 'shaped' by judicious timing of food reward. In a similar way one person can manipulate another's conversation by appropriate use of social rewards. Listening to a subject talking on a particular topic, an experimenter can influence the style, topic, and even the use of particular classes of words, such as plural nouns, by saying 'good' or making some other sign of approval at the appropriate moments. Under these conditions the subjects tend to use the rewarded items more frequently. When such rewards are withheld the subject starts to change the topic or style of

E

his monologue, thus demonstrating the phenomenon of 'extinction', familiar to students of animal behaviour.

Let us now turn from the study of individuals to the study of people in groups. It is useful to distinguish between a collection of unacquainted people and a group of people who depend upon one another to play distinctive roles in the pursuit of common interests or goals. Social psychologists usually reserve the word 'group' for the latter. Although it is possible to study groups by simple observation alone, it is common for social psychologists to employ confederates who become part of a group and play a crucial role in the conduct of the experiment, without the knowledge of the true subjects. For example, in a study of behaviour standardisation, subjects were asked to say which of two lines was the shorter. The collaborators of the experimenter answered first, and it was found that, when they said that line A was shorter than line B, though it was in fact clearly longer, there was a strong tendency for the subjects also to say that line A was shorter. Standardisation of behaviour and conformity due to group pressure are typical findings of social psychologists, and are human traits often exploited by advertisers.

Another common method of studying group behaviour is the use of questionnaires. Because of the inherent pitfalls in this method, the design of questionnaires has become a specialised field and will be dealt with at length in Chapter 9. Questionnaires completed by mothers of 5–6 year olds suggested, for example, that the more aggressive children tend to come from homes where rules about aggressiveness are permissive, but where punishment for acting aggressively is heavy. Conversely, the less aggressive children are confronted by strong rules about aggression, but non-punitive means of dealing with it. Before accepting such conclusions, however, one would have to be sure that there was no alternative interpretation of the results. For example, permissive mothers may differ from strict mothers in what they regard as aggressive behaviour; the questionnaire may have revealed more about the personality of the mothers than the aggressiveness of the children.

The use of social surveys and questionnaires brings social psychology close to the social sciences, such as sociology and social anthropology. Anthropologists have long studied the behaviour of peoples in their natural environment. However, these studies are usually concerned with behavioural artefacts, such as the institutions of marriage and government, rather than with the behaviour itself. Although the study of institutions can throw light on the psychology of the individual, this type of work does not at present fall within the scope of behavioural science. Nevertheless, it would be a pity if psychologists ignored studies which might be able to contribute to their understanding of human behaviour.

8 Studying Humans in the Laboratory

Human experimental psychology is an extensive field of study and rather than cataloguing all its branches we will select a few topics for more detailed description.

Visual perception is a subject that has long interested psychologists and many investigators have made use of optical devices which distort the normal visual field. For example, if a subject wears spectacles fitted with laterally displacing prisms, objects will appear to be displaced either to the left or right of their true position, as shown in Figure 9. Asked to point at a target the subject points incorrectly, especially if he cannot see his hand and so guide it on to the target. If the subject is then allowed to see his hand he sees the amount by which his pointing was in error. Under these conditions most subjects rapidly adapt to the situation and correct their error. If, after adaptation, the prisms are removed and the subject immediately points at the target, there is usually an error in pointing, but this time to the side opposite to the original displacement. This phenomenon is called the after-effect.

Four stages of adaptation to laterally displacing prisms are illustrated in Figure 10. The whole phenomenon can be demonstrated in less than five minutes, thus showing that there is a rapid recalibration somewhere within the visual-motor co-ordination system. Where and how does the recalibration take place? This is the type of problem which interests laboratory investigators of human behaviour and will be used to illustrate some of the principles involved in their experiments.

The first problem is to devise a standardised method of testing and in particular it is important that subjects are tested in the same bodily position. Figure 10 shows an arrangement which fulfils these requirements. The subject sits with his shoulders parallel to the row of targets, so that the direction of pointing can be measured accurately as the angle between the arm and the line of the shoulders. In addition the subject's head is usually fixed in a constant position by asking him to bite on a bar. He cannot see his arms and the targets are viewed against a uniform background. To ensure that the subject

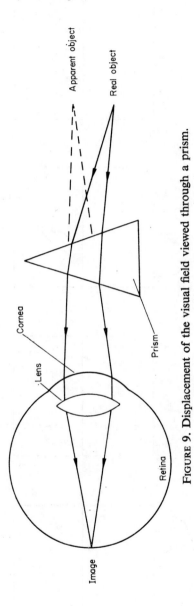

FIGURE 9. Displacement of the visual field viewed through a prism.

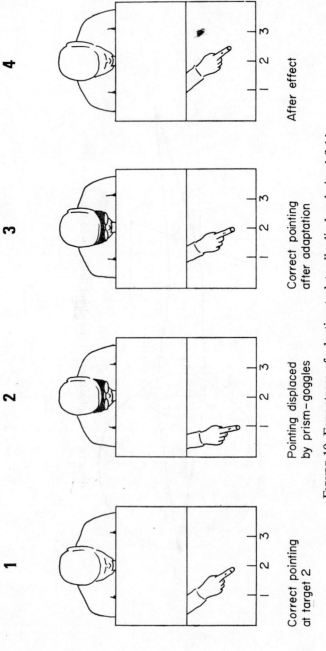

FIGURE 10. Four stages of adaption to laterally displaced visual field.

From 'Vision and Touch', Irvin Roch and Charles S. Hains, *Scientific American*, May 1967.

does not develop a stereotyped response several individually marked targets are presented and the experimenter calls out which target is to be pointed at. After each try the subject returns his arm to a standard position.

At the beginning of each experimental session the subject's normal pointing accuracy is determined by asking him to point at various targets a number of times. Prism goggles are then fitted and the subject is again asked to point at the targets. Only when the act of pointing is complete is the subject allowed to see his finger and note his error. Initially most subjects point at an angle corresponding to the angular deviation of the visual target induced by the prisms, but gradually they correct their error. A criterion for the completion of adaptation has to be chosen, and this is usually ten to twenty consecutively correct trials.

A number of hypotheses have been advanced to explain this type of adaptation. The experiment to be outlined here was devised by Brian Craske to test the hypothesis that adaption consists of a change in the 'felt position' of the arm. In other words, the subject who normally feels his arm to be in a certain angular relationship to his body has this felt-relationship changed by the repeated observation that there is a discrepancy between the seen and the felt position of the arm during training. The hypothesis implies that the discrepancy causes a recalibration of the felt position of the arm, such that the discrepancy is reduced to zero.

To test this hypothesis Brian Craske first of all ensured that each subject could locate the position of one arm by pointing to it with the other hand. The arm ultimately to be used for pointing at targets, say the left arm, was clamped underneath a horizontal sheet of opaque glass, in a fixed position relative to the shoulder, with the elbow joint straight. The right arm could rest on the top of the glass sheet, but the subject was unable to see the left arm clamped underneath. When the experimenter touched the left arm with a glass rod, at the wrist, elbow, or shoulder, the subject was required to indicate the place that had been touched by pointing with the index finger of his right hand to the corresponding position on the upper surface of the glass. After the subject had pointed correctly ten times, his left hand was removed from the clamps and used to point at targets, which were viewed through prisms in the manner described above. When the subject had adapted to the prismatic displacement and was pointing correctly, his left arm was again clamped under the glass sheet, and the arm-location test repeated. The results were in line with the hypothesis; whereas subjects had been able to locate arm position correctly before adaptation to prismatic displacement, after adaptation they made an error of judgment related to the displacement of the visual field induced by the prisms. In other words, the subject made a small error when his shoulder was touched by the experimenter, a larger error when his elbow was touched, and an even larger error when his wrist was indicated, precisely the result that would be expected if the angular 'felt position' of the left arm had been changed during the course of adaptation to prismatic displacement. However, the angular difference between the indicated positions of the arm before and after adaptation was not as great as the angular displacement to which the subject had adapted, indicating that the 'felt position' of the arm is not the only mechanism used in adaptation to displacement of the visual field.

This study illustrates two general points about experimental procedure. The first is the careful use of controls; the need to take precautions against alternative interpretations of the results. Thus both the arm-location task, and the adaptation task are based on comparison of results obtained before and after experimental manipulation. The carefully designed set of procedures guards against the possibility that some subjects could have a pre-existing pointing, or arm-location bias. The experimental design is such that each subject acts as his own control and enough subjects are tested to give statistically reliable results. This situation therefore differs from that outlined in Chapter 5 in which control groups of animals were used.

The second point is that subjects are required to demonstrate behaviourally whatever change has been induced by the experimental procedure, instead of being asked what they *thought* had occurred. Thus in the pointing experiment described above, the subject may well believe that a purely visual change has occurred, which was indeed the reaction of the first experimental psychologists who used themselves as subjects in the investigation of this phenomenon. Having thus illustrated the unreliability of introspection, we can now turn to an area of investigation in which the distinction between awareness and reality is even more important.

Introspection suggests that it is difficult to think about more than one thing at a time, but that some activities, such as walking, which require little thought, can be carried out at the same time as other activities. To the early psychologists who sought to analyse thought processes subjectively, our limited attention was obviously an important factor. However, even those psychologists who had real insight into such problems had no way of showing that their suppositions were correct, and for some time this type of problem was shelved.

The development of a more objective psychology opened up new avenues of approach, and one of the early informative experiments was reported by Colin Cherry in 1953. He presented his subjects with two speakers simultaneously, asking them to listen to only one of them. To ensure that the subject concentrated on one speaker, he was required to repeat the words two or three words after he heard them. Asked what he had noticed about the speech to which he was not attending, the subject could recall very little. He was aware that the speaker was a woman, but failed to notice that she had switched from English to German. This experiment demonstrates the operation of a process of selective attention which is commonly used in everyday life; in listening to one speaker at a party for example. The experiment reveals little about the mechanism of selective attention, although it does show that both speakers must have made some physical impact on the subject.

As a result of her investigations into this type of phenomenon, Anne Triesman has proposed that there are three main types of selective attention. The first is similar to that discussed in Chapter 5, where an example of selective attention in animals was discussed in relation to the process of discrimination learning. The subject attends to particular aspects of the stimulus situation and ignores others. Thus a rat may attend to the brightness difference between two stimuli and ignore the shape difference. Similarly, a human may attend to the spelling of words and ignore their meaning. In the second type of attention a particular source of stimulation, such as a particular speaker, is selected and everything possible about the stimuli coming from this source is analysed, all other sources being ignored. The third type of attention is concerned with all stimuli connected with a particular outcome, or goal. Thus an animal might search for any stimulus connected with food, or a human go shopping for a hat without having any particular colour or style in mind.

It is helpful to think of sensory information as being 'filtered' through a number of 'analysers' each of which distinguishes between specific characteristics of the stimulus. Thus there might be an analyser for colour, one for shape, and another for brightness. The various types of attention can be distinguished by the way in which the sensory information is sorted through the analysers. For example, in attending to particular aspects of the stimulus, the analysers would be arranged in parallel, as shown in Figure 11 (*a*), but only one, or perhaps a few, would operate at any one time. Thus we can attend to either shape or colour, but not to both simultaneously. Alternatively, in attending to sources of stimulation, the analysers would be arranged in series, each passing only a limited amount of information to the next, as shown in Figure 11(*b*). The two types of mechanism probably operate simultaneously, and are followed by a third which is responsible for the analysis of meaning.

Experiments with humans have concentrated mainly on selection between sources of stimulation, as this appears to be the most important type of attention in man. Thus Anne Triesman suggests that in attending to different aspects of speech, where the analysers are arranged in parallel, the number of speakers heard should make no difference to the efficiency of attending, as measured by reporting the message from one speaker. The subject would ignore differences in loudness, pitch, etc., between the speakers and could concentrate on the message itself. On the other hand, if the analysers are arranged in series, the subject has to distinguish relevant from irrelevant sources before he can attend to the message. In experiments in which recorded messages were presented simultaneously through microphones to different ears, Anne Triesman found that subjects had more difficulty in attending to one speaker when distracted by another than when they were played the same total number of words from one speaker. When a foreign language was introduced from the same source as the relevant speech, subjects were more distracted the better they knew the language, but were not distracted by a foreign language coming from a different source. These results indicate that the subjects attend to many aspects from a single source, and few from other sources. However, it can be shown that some simple aspects of a message from an irrelevant source can also affect the subjects' performance. Subjects asked to tap when hearing the word 'tap' given by two speakers while listening only to one speaker, missed many cues from the irrelevant speaker. But subjects in a similar experiment, who were asked to tap on hearing a physical pip, were able to respond to pips provided by both sources.

In this type of study the relationship between hypothesis and

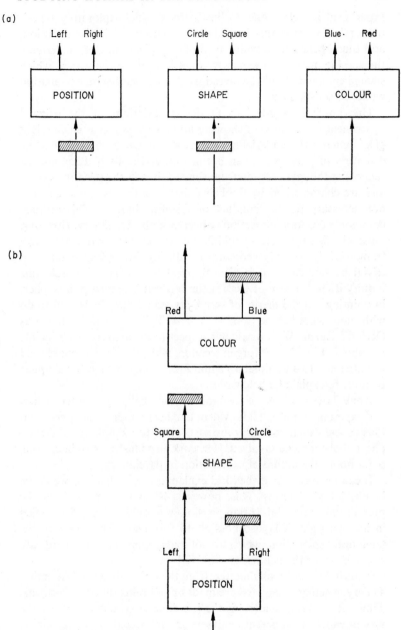

FIGURE 11. Two possible arrangements of analysers, resulting in two types of selective attention.

experiment is a close one. Colin Cherry's initial exploratory experiment raised specific questions about the nature of selective attention, and thus opened up a whole field of investigation. But, underlying the specific questions are general questions about the way in which such phenomena should be investigated, and what type of explanation would be satisfactory.

One possible approach is to devise variations of the original experiment in the hope of showing up new phenomena which might give a clue to the underlying processes. The danger here is that the discovery of phenomena can become an end in itself. Phenomenist schools of thought crop up from time to time in the scientific world, and are characterised by the belief that hypothetical constructs are not necessary for the conduct of scientific inquiry. This attitude commonly occurs as a reaction to over-complicated theory. However, most scientists try to steer a middle course, believing that a theoretical framework is not only necessary for distinguishing important from trivial phenomena, but is also essential to the nature of scientific inquiry itself. William of Occam, the thirteenth-century philosopher, in pointing out the merits of simplicity stated that, 'It is vain to do with more what can be done with fewer'. This maxim is known as Occam's Razor. With particular respect to behaviour, this principle is embodied in Lloyd Morgan's canon, which states that one should not attribute to an animal a mental faculty higher than the simplest possible to explain its behaviour.

Anne Triesman's work maintains a nice balance between theory and experiment, though it is evident that her hypotheses are parsimonious to the extent that they are at present too simple for the complicated phenomena involved. Her work also illustrates an interesting point about the nature of explanation in psychology.

It can be argued that the ideal explanation of behaviour would be in physiological terms. This, however, is far from possible at the present time, and whilst brain physiology should certainly be studied in its own right, it is also possible to formulate other types of behavioural explanation, which do not make reference to the hardware responsible for the behaviour observed.

Thus it does not really matter, from the point of view of Attention Theory, whether 'analysers' are made up of brain cells or of electronic components. What matters is the job done by each analyser and the way in which the different analysers are connected. So in explaining man's limited capacity to handle incoming information, an abstract 'mechanism' consisting of interlocking information channels can be constructed, and can provide as valid an explanation as the description of a mechanism in terms of hardware. Indeed, this method is sometimes used by engineers in preference to the circuit (hardware) diagram of a complex electronic machine. The psychologist, therefore, need not wait upon the physiologist to describe the hardware responsible for behaviour, but can proceed on the basis that behaviour can be explained at a level which assumes that physiological mechanisms capable of carrying out the required operations will be discovered. The task of the psychologist is to determine what the required operations are.

9 Asking People Questions

Asking people questions may be the most obvious way of investigating human behaviour, but it is by no means the most straightforward. Verbal interchange is so much a part of everyday life that an investigator using this method is especially prone to the type of egocentric outlook described in Chapters 1 and 6, and can easily relapse into subjective interpretation of the situation. He needs, therefore, to be even more scrupulous about maintaining an objective approach than workers using other types of behavioural investigation Verbal questioning has thus become a most refined tool of psychology, and one which is most easily open to misuse.

Historically, it is probable that nineteenth-century sociologists were the first to use systematic questionnaires. Charles Booth, a rich Liverpool shipowner, conducted a survey of the working-class population of London in 1886. Booth collected his data indirectly, from School Attendance Officers and the like. A decade later Benjamin Rowntree started a study of poverty in York. Rowntree improved on Booth's technique by (1) obtaining his data directly from the families by using interviewers; (2) aiming to obtain data from every wage-earning family in York; and (3) classifying his information into rigorously defined categories. In 1912 Arthur Bowley made a study of working-class conditions in Reading, and was the first to use a definite sampling procedure.

The reasoning behind sampling is that a judgment can be made about the nature of a population or commodity by inspecting only a small part of it. The wine taster does not need to drink the whole bottle to form a judgment about a particular wine. Because he believes that the wine in the bottle is homogeneous, he can confidently expect that a sample will adequately represent the whole. However, the student of human behaviour cannot be so confident as human populations are not well mixed, but tend to consist of groups of people with similar attributes. Thus it would not be legitimate to make a judgment about people in general from a study of university students, unless there was reason to believe that the attributes being studied were equally common in the population as a whole. There-

78

fore, it is necessary to design the sampling procedure in advance, rather than take samples in a haphazard fashion.

There are two principles which underlie all sample design: (1) the need to avoid bias in the selection procedure, and (2) the need to achieve maximum precision for a given outlay of resources. Bias in the selection procedure can be avoided by sampling the population at random. But to ensure a random sample it is necessary to have a sample frame, which consists of a list, index, or other record, with reference to which the random sampling can be achieved. If the sampling frame does not cover the population adequately, errors will arise due to non-random sampling. For example, a telephone directory would not constitute an adequate sample frame as it excludes much of the population in the lower income bracket. Care must be taken to ensure that the selection is not consciously or unconsciously influenced by human choice. It has been repeatedly shown that the human investigator is unsatisfactory for making random selections, and that he tends, usually unconsciously, to favour certain population units. It is essential to ensure randomness by a means independent of human judgment, and generally the members of the population are numbered and the sample frame constructed from a table of random numbers. In such a way a social investigator might be provided with a list of people to visit and interview. However, it is probable that he will not be able to obtain information from all the people on the list. Some he may be unable to find, and others may refuse to co-operate. Errors introduced in this way must be taken into account when the results are evaluated. The advantage of random sampling over other methods of choosing a part of a population is that, when estimates of the population characteristics are made from the sample results, the precision of these estimates can also be gauged from the sample results themselves by the use of sophisticated statistical techniques. The sampling method is widely used in areas beyond that for which it was originally devised, for example, to check the quality of factory goods.

Having decided on a certain sampling procedure, the investigator must then decide how the information is to be obtained from the subjects. Questions can be asked verbally by an interviewer, or by means of a written questionnaire. Although the former is probably the more reliable procedure, the latter is more economical; as Marie Jahoda has pointed out, 'Questionnaires can be sent through the mail; interviewers cannot'.

Although questionnaires have certain obvious advantages, they are also subject to limitations. It is difficult to avoid ambiguity except in the most simple questions. Answers have to be taken at face value, and spontaneous answers cannot be distinguished from thought-out answers. Different answers cannot be treated as independent, because the subject can see all the questions before answering any one of them. Finally, it is relatively easy for subjects to fail to answer a question, or to answer irresponsibly. When this happens it is difficult to know whether the non-responding part of the population is representative of the population as a whole, or whether they have attributes not shared by the rest of the population. In the latter case the sample of adequate responses cannot be taken as truly random; bias therefore is difficult to avoid. These limitations place severe constraints on the design of questionnaires, which need to be simple and straightforward in layout. Much more variability and subtlety of design is possible when interviewers are employed.

The interview may have a variety of roles in the design of a study. It may be employed during the early stages to help identify the relevant parameters of the study. It may be used as the main instrument of data collection, or to clarify findings which emerge from the use of other techniques. The interview is a flexible tool which can be altered to suit its role in the study. For example, for data collection a formal interview is generally better, but pre- and post-test interviews are sometimes informal.

In formal interviewing questions are asked and answers recorded in a standardised manner. Generally the questions will have been decided upon in advance of the interview, and asked in the same order for all subjects. Formal interviews are aimed at obtaining maximum reliability, that is, the extent to which the same interview given to the same subjects by different interviewers would give the same results. The conduct of an informal interview is largely in the hands of the interviewer, who can alter his questions to suit the situation and can generally probe deeply into the meaning of the answers given by the respondent. Informal interviews generally yield less reliable, though more valid, answers. This is because the same question may have different meanings for different people, and the informal interview makes it possible to ensure that the subject understands the intended meaning of the question. However, as it has been shown that variation in the wording of questions can have marked effects upon the answers obtained, great care must be taken over their phrasing.

The objective in wording questions is to provide a set of stimuli to which the subject will give a relevant response. As with all such studies, the first task is to ensure that the stimulus is within the stimulus-range of the subject. It is clearly no good asking a question in terms that the subject cannot understand. Research workers are often tempted to translate their objectives into questions too directly. For example, if the investigator wishes to know why the subject behaved in a certain manner, it would not be good practice to ask him 'Why did you do that?' As we saw in Chapter 2, in asking 'why' questions about behaviour there are many frames of reference to be taken into account. Clearly the subject cannot know in advance what kind of answer is expected of him. Thus, when a mother is asked why she talks baby-talk to her child, she may answer 'Because it is good for him', an answer in terms of function; or 'Because I love him', an answer in terms of mechanism. If the investigator wishes to know about the motivation of the behaviour, he must phrase the questions in a less direct way.

Whether the research worker devises a standard set of questions in advance, or composes the questions as he goes along, he must try to avoid the common pitfalls in phrasing his questions. Many obvious pitfalls, such as ambiguous or vague questions, are in practice not easy to avoid, because many subtle interpretations can be put upon an apparently simple and straightforward question. For example, the question 'How often do you smoke cigarettes?' is both vague and ambiguous. Firstly, there is no indication of the time scale to which the answer should refer. Thus the answer 'I smoke cigarettes every day' could cover up the fact that the subject smokes a cigarette every hour. Secondly, there is no indication of the quantity of smoking involved. Thus the answer 'I smoke twice a day' could mean that the subject smokes two cigarettes a day, or that he smokes half a cigarette in the morning and half in the afternoon. 'How many cigarettes do you generally smoke in a day?' would be a better question. It is important also to avoid leading questions, which by content or structure lead the subject in the direction of a certain answer. The question 'Are promotions in your office usually based on merit?' may, by presenting one possible answer, prevent the subject from thinking of others. The interviewer should either remind the subject of all the possibilities, or of none of them. In the latter case the question could be 'What are promotions in your office usually based on?' This question is an open question, which allows the subject to

F

answer freely. The alternative would be a closed, or pre-coded question, in which the subject is presented with a list of possible answers. For example, in answering the question 'Are promotions in your office usually based on (a) merit, (b) age, (c) social status, (d) years of service?' he may simply be required to tick the appropriate answer. The danger here is omission of possible answers from the list. An 'others' category can be introduced to avoid this difficulty, thus moving towards a more open type of question. Closed questions are generally considered to be more reliable in collecting factual information, but open questions often yield more valid information about matters of opinion or motivation. Asking questions about the latter is a particularly delicate matter, and special techniques are often employed in interviewing when the subject matter is likely to arouse resistance. A common technique is the use of an indirect rather than a direct method of questioning.

The rationale behind indirect methods is that they will provide relevant information without the subject being fully aware of the implications of his replies. A typical example is the use of a 'projective' question, which usually refers to someone other than the respondent. Thus instead of asking 'How do you feel when your father refuses to let you stay out late?' the subject is asked 'How do you think young people feel when their fathers refuse to let them stay out late?' Subjects are often more willing to answer questions about other people than they are to answer questions about themselves. The interviewer hopes that the subject will project his own feelings or beliefs on to the people mentioned in the question. The difficulty here is to be sure that such projection has taken place. It has sometimes been found that subjects give different answers to direct and projective questions and the problem is to know which represents their true attitude.

Another indirect method is the error-choice method, in which subjects are asked to choose from a variety of possible answers an answer to a factual question. All the answers provided are incorrect and the type of error that the subject chooses is supposed to reflect his attitude to the question. In many psychological tests subjects are asked to complete stories, arguments or pictures which are presented to them during the interview. Such methods are frequently used to assess attitude.

All methods of interviewing are open to a certain amount of bias due to poor wording of questions, but bias can also occur as a result of other factors, such as the role relationships in the interview. An interview in which the interviewer is present in person is very different from a remotely conducted interview, such as a telephone conversation. In a personal interview the behaviour of the subject will be influenced by his attitude to the interviewer as a person; interviewees are known to be particularly sensitive to the interviewer's apparent social status. Although the interviewer must occupy some role, he should attempt to make his position as neutral as possible. In other words, he should adopt a role that is unlikely to influence the subject's attitude to the interview. For example, if the respondent were a civil servant, it would be inappropriate for the interviewer to appear in the role of a civil servant, as the subject might interpret the interview as relevant to his promotion prospects, even if the subject matter of the interview were totally irrelevant to this. The research interviewer should take particular care to be outside the subject's social hierarchy and irrelevant to his personal life. The situation is different, of course, when the interview has some practical aim, such as assessing candidates for a job.

It has been shown that interviewers are generally more successful in obtaining information if they appear to be reasonably knowledgeable about the subject matter of the interview. Thus interviewers working with respondents from the underworld must know some underworld jargon to gain the confidence of the respondents. On the other hand, the interviewer must not appear to be too knowledgeable and must appear to need and want information from the respondent. The interviewer must also be careful how he responds to the subject's replies, he must take care not to 'reward' the subject by appearing to approve of certain types of reply, by nodding his head or saying 'How interesting', for example. On the other hand, if the interviewer is too unresponsive, the subject is liable to become frustrated or bored. These factors are particularly important in the informal type of interview, but are also relevant to interviews with pre-prepared questions.

It should now be clear that questionnaires and interviews are liable to many sources of error, and they may well appear to be unreliable when compared with non-verbal methods of obtaining information about behaviour. However, much depends upon the way in which the results are handled, and as long as the investigator is aware of the pitfalls there is no reason why these methods should not be as reliable as any other.

The first step in considering the analysis of results is to determine the most suitable level of measurement. Four levels of measurement may be distinguished: (1) Measurement at a *nominal* level is attained when the data is classified into a number of equivalent categories. For example, asked what type of tobacco they prefer, a group of subjects might yield the following result: cigarettes 70%, cigars 20%, pipe tobacco 10%. These categories differ only in the quality of the tobacco smoked, there being no quantitative distinction. (2) An *ordinal* scale distinguishes between categories on quantitative grounds. Thus people might be asked whether they (*a*) very much, (*b*) slightly, or (*c*) do not prefer cigarettes to other forms of tobacco. In this case it is possible to rank (*a*), (*b*) and (*c*) on a scale of increasing preference, although no proper units of measurement are used. (3) An *interval* scale goes one step further in that it is possible to say, not only that one item is greater, or more preferred, than another, but by how much. Such a scale is characterised by a common and constant unit of measurement. The zero point and unit of measurement are arbitrary, and the ratio of any two intervals is independent of the unit of measurement. These points can be verified by consideration of the centigrade and Fahrenheit scales for measuring temperature, which are typical interval scales. (4) Finally, the *ratio* scale has all the characteristics of an interval scale, and in addition has a true zero point. For example, in measuring weight, the gramme scale and the ounce scale both have the same zero point. This, the strongest level of measurement, permits the use of any type of mathematical operation. It is important to realise that, as the levels of measurement employed become weaker, so the range of permissible mathematical operations is reduced. Therefore, the scientist who wishes to make the maximum use of his results should always strive towards the strongest level of measurement. The analysis of the results of the interview-type of study are often invalidated by improper use of statistical analysis, which is due to failure to relate the type of statistic to the level of measurement employed.

Achieving a nominal or ordinal level of measurement is a relatively straightforward matter, but the interval and ratio scales are not so easy to attain. Various types of 'rating scale' are employed to this end, of which the 'scalogram' is a typical example. Subjects are presented with a series of related questions to which they have to give yes–no answers. For example:

1. Do you smoke more than twenty cigarettes a day?

2. Do you smoke more than fifteen cigarettes a day?
3. Do you smoke more than ten cigarettes a day?

Only four patterns of answer are possible, assuming that accurate answers are given.

	Says yes to item			Says no to item		
Score	1	2	3	1	2	3
3	×	×	×			
2		×	×	×		
1			×	×	×	
0				×	×	×

The scores obtained from this method can be represented on a ratio scale as long as the answers are scalable to this extent. The perfect scale implies that a person who answers 'yes' to a given question will obtain a higher score than a person who answers 'no'. The extent to which a scale approximates to this ideal can be measured by a *coefficient of reproducibility*, which is the percentage of responses that can be correctly predicted from knowledge of the total score. Pilot tests can be conducted to determine the set of questions that give the best coefficient of reproducibility.

Having obtained an appropriate level of measurement, the results can be analysed statistically in the same manner as the results from any other type of study. In particular, statistics can be used to detect sampling errors and to make predictions about the nature of the population as a whole. However, statistics can only be used to determine the reliability of the results and conclusions. The validity of these will depend upon the scientist's ability to ask questions which are relevant to the theoretical background of the study. As with all scientific progress, theory and experiment must go hand in hand.

10 Behaviour and Everyday Life

In this book we have been primarily concerned with the aims and methods of behavioural research. The reader may well have wondered about the relevance of such research to everyday life.

First of all, it is important to realise that, as an academic discipline, the study of behaviour is in its infancy. Therefore, it would be naive at this stage to expect great insights into the behaviour of ourselves or our fellows. Indeed, if we cannot adequately explain how a rat learns the shortest route through a maze, how can we expect to account for the behaviour of the most complex organism yet evolved? What, then, can we expect to learn from the study of behaviour that is relevant to everyday life?

An important contribution of behavioural research is the development of a rigorous scientific approach to the study of behaviour. For example, Sigmund Freud's assertion that an instinct is the sum of psychic energy which imparts direction to psychological processes would not today be regarded as a scientifically meaningful statement. Psychic energy cannot be investigated experimentally, and since by definition it derives from the instincts, its existence cannot be verified independently of the instinct defined by it. But the statement that an instinct is a genetically controlled predisposition to behave in a certain manner is open to experimental investigation, and can be verified in terms independent of the definition. In other words, behaviour patterns can be classified objectively by means of this definition of instinct.

Progress has also been made in the techniques of behavioural investigation. Even if we do not know how a rat learns a route through a maze, we do know the necessary conditions for the behaviour. Thus the rat must be rewarded on reaching the goal and motivated to obtain the reward, if it is to demonstrate its learning ability. Many of the techniques of behaviour science have direct application to everyday life. For example, the techniques of operant conditioning have been used to employ pigeons to sort out defective components in a factory. The components are paraded past a window through which they are viewed by the pigeon. The bird pecks at a key when it sees a defective component, and this causes the pigeon to be rewarded and the component to be rejected from the batch. In order to maintain the behaviour over long periods, batches are seeded with known defective and satisfactory components, the bird being rewarded and punished appropriately for pecking at these. Research on operant conditioning in animals has also led to the development of teaching machines for use by students learning prescribed material, such as elementary mathematics. The student is presented with a question to which he chooses one of a number of alternative answers by pressing the appropriate button. He is then told whether his answer is correct, and if it is, the next question is presented; if not, an earlier question in the sequence is presented, so that the student repeats that part of the routine. This method allows each student to learn at his own pace, and has proved very effective for certain kinds of learning material.

Many of the applications of behavioural research come directly from applied research rather than from the academic study of behaviour. For example, a large amount of work has been carried out on the peculiar types of 'fatigue' experienced during tasks involving long periods of vigilance, such as watching a radar screen. Similarly, the effect of loud noise on human performance, and the efficient design of instrument panels, are typical examples of practical problems which are investigated in laboratories of applied psychology. The development of aptitude tests, and other methods of personnel selection, also result from work carried out with a practical end in view. Although academic research is usually aimed at the basic principles of behaviour, rather than at particular practical problems, contributions to the latter sometimes occur as by-products of the line of inquiry. Conversely, applied psychologists often make discoveries of academic interest, so that the two types of work tend to merge.

During the last twenty years psychologists have become increasingly involved in industry, education and medicine. Knowledge of behaviour is particularly relevant to these aspects of everyday life; in education, methods of teaching and child development are the main areas of interest; in medicine, psychologists are engaged in clinical diagnosis and in therapy. Psychologists are employed in the armed services, in prisons, in advertising agencies, and in industry as personnel officers. Although a large amount of research work is devoted to practical problems in these areas, there is an unfortunate tendency for academic theories to be applied prematurely. Whenever scientific theories are carried over into everyday life, there should always be a thorough experimental investigation at the practical level. A good example of this procedure is the current experimental testing of discrimination learning in children, which is following up on theories of discrimination learning based on animal studies. In this case the results have been extremely fruitful. Too often, however, theories are applied to everyday life, without any attempt at further verification. This procedure is particularly common, and particularly dangerous, when applied to therapy.

It is often argued that the therapist is faced with mentally sick people who cannot wait for the scientist to discover the root causes of the trouble. This is a situation which has long existed in medicine, not only in the field of mental illness. The remedy lies in standard clinical practice, which relies on past experience of diagnosis and treatment, and not on academic theories about the system. A doctor who gives a patient an aspirin need not know how aspirins cause relief; he needs to make a correct diagnosis and to know that treatment with aspirins brings relief without causing undesirable side effects. In the days of herbal remedies, people used willow bark to relieve head-aches; research has shown that willow bark contains salicylic acid, the main constituent of aspirin. The application of scientific research to medical practice is a relatively recent development, and the advance-ment of medicine has come, not only from scientific discoveries, but also from improved techniques of clinical observation and treatment.

Sound clinical practice should form the basis of therapeutic work, particularly when little is known about the system responsible for the illness, as is the case with most mental illnesses. The worst possible approach is to base treatment on metaphysical theories. Just as medical treatment was particularly ineffective when based on re-ligious belief and superstition, modern psychoanalytic therapy, based on the essentially metaphysical theories of Freud, Jung and Adler, is little better. It is not surprising, therefore, that the success rate of psychoanalysis is about equivalent to that of medieval medicine. Behaviour therapy, based on the application of conditioning theory, claims a greater success rate, but suffers from rigid adherence to insufficiently verified theories about behaviour. The best hope for the mentally sick person in this century is to go to a consultant with medical training and a sound experience in clinical practice, which, thankfully, the majority of British psychiatrists have. To expect the science of behaviour to have important things to say today about human mental processes is to ask it to run before it can walk.

Further Reading

Chapter 1

Charles Singer, *A Short History of Scientific Ideas to 1900*. Oxford Paperbacks, O.U.P., 1962

Desmond Morris, *The Naked Ape*, Jonathan Cape, London, 1967

Chapter 2

Niko Tinbergen, *Animal Behaviour*, Life Nature Library, 1966

A. J. Ayer, *Man as a Subject for Science*, Auguste Comte Memorial Lecture 6, The Athlone Press, 1964

Chapter 3

Aubrey Manning, *An Introduction to Animal Behaviour*, Edward Arnold, London, 1967

Katharine Tansley, *Vision in Vertebrates*, Science Paperbacks 11, 1965

Chapter 4

Charles Darwin, *The Expression of the Emotions in Man and Animals*, Phoenix Books, The University of Chicago Press, 1965

Niko Tinbergen, *Social Behaviour in Animals*, Science Paperbacks 1, 1965

Chapter 5

Donald Broadbent, *Behaviour*, Eyre & Spottiswoode, London, 1961

Chapter 6

Konrad Lorenz, *On Aggression*, Methuen, 1963

Gustav Schenk, *The History of Man*, Basic Science Series, Chr. Belser Verlag, Stuttgart, 1961

Chapter 7

Michael Argyle, *The Psychology of Interpersonal Behaviour*, Penguin Books (Pelican), 1966

Chapter 8

George Miller, *Psychology, The Science of Mental Life*, Penguin Books (Pelican), 1962

Chapter 9

Colin Cherry, *On Human Communication*, Science Editions, Wiley, 1961

Index